This book is an honest, down-to-earth story of a journey through the pain of childlessness – frustration in the efforts of overcoming this ache and an eventual coming to terms with life as it is, rather than the way we want or expect it to be.

Malcolm and Nick, who share the writing of this story, have done so, not out of a sense of bravado, but simply because by doing so, they hope they might help others in similar circumstances.

It certainly meets a need, in an age when babies are produced or aborted on demand – sometimes easily available to those who don't want them, but denied to those who desperately long for them.

This story is not a pious, meek acceptance of the status quo, but explodes with full-on emotions of the ache of unfulfilled expectations and interestingly, from both the male and female perspectives. Although comparatively few of us have had to face this particular set of circumstances, most, if not all could identify with the emotions of anger, pain and despair so honestly explained here. Through many Biblical parallels, the book shows that although this story does not have the 'happily ever after' ending we always hope for, it reveals the power of trust in a God who teaches us that our future is assured and that the ultimate ending is happy for those who believe.

It's OK to Cry is an apt title, because believe me, you will!

Fiona Castle

This book ⋯ ⋯ rds, 'I am classed b⋯ ⋯tile, I am

classed by society as childless, I am classed by God as a daughter – a son, an heir, precious, treasured, dearly loved.' Here is a moving and startlingly real account of one couple's struggle with deep pain and disappointment, and of the faith on which they draw to see them through. It is written for the sake of other couples like them and deserves to be widely recommended.

Dr Nigel G. Wright
Principal, Spurgeon's College, London

'This book is not for the faint-hearted. It's written for those who are suffering the intense pain of bereavement in childlessness. It's raw, real and compulsory reading for those who want to enter in and understand something of the pain some childless couples are called to endure. Sometimes God miraculously answers prayers for a child, but the complete answer hasn't come yet for Malcolm and Nick. *It's OK to Cry* is about a couple who experience the untold heartache of not seeing their desires realized and who live to tell the tale, and rejoice in the Lord.'

Lyndon Bowring
CARE

IT'S OK TO
CRY
**FINDING HOPE
WHEN STRUGGLING
WITH INFERTILITY
& MISCARRIAGE**

MALCOLM &
NICK CAMERON

CHRISTIAN FOCUS

Scripture quotations taken from the HOLY BIBLE, NEW INTERNATIONAL VERSION. Copyright © 1973, 1978, 1984 by International Bible Society. Used by permission of Hodder & Stoughton Publishers, A member of the Hodder Headline Group. All rights reserved. "NIV" is a registered trademark of International Bible Society.

10 9 8 7 6 5 4 3 2 1

ISBN 1-84550077-6

Published in 2005
by
Christian Focus Publications, Ltd.,
Geanies House, Fearn, Ross-shire,
IV20 1TW, Scotland

www.christianfocus.com

Cover design by Alister MacInnes

Printed and bound by
Nørhaven Paperback A/S, Denmark

Contents

Dedication

There are simply too many people that I could dedicate this book to – our massive family, friends, colleagues, so many people who Malcolm and I are so thankful to – you know who you are – thank you!

The fellowship at Lansdowne who have exceeded themselves in loving us – "you're lovely, you are."

To those at Christian Focus who from the day we met them encouraged us to encourage others – bless you!

But really this book is dedicated to the lone couple who are heart-broken, living in disappointment, struggling to find hope, to those who sit in silence, those who weep frequently – we walk a dark pathway – be encouraged Malcolm and I have found hope in that darkness!

This book is also dedicated to those that are related to, or minister to, heart-broken childless couples – may your lives be touched <u>by</u> Jesus so that you can <u>be</u> Jesus to the hurting.

But most of all, this entire book is dedicated to my faithful Lord and my awesome God – the One who has been with us in the darkest hour, who has recorded every tear that I've ever shed, who has touched my broken heart. You have sustained me, met me, forgiven me, comforted me, sheltered me, guided me, saved me, walked with me, loved me unconditionally – you have given me a new song to sing – to you belongs eternal praise!

FOREWORD

I am privileged to write a foreword for this book. Seldom does a book come along nowadays from someone generally unknown to the world which still gets published. But this book deserves to be read by many, many Christians. It will be deeply treasured by all who read it. This is because so many of us have experienced the equivalent of the pain described so poignantly and graphically in the book.

Whereas the story told in this book relates to a couple's profound grief over remaining childless, which all may not relate to, we all have something in our lives that we wanted so desperately and had to be resigned to the fact that it would not come along. This book addresses such a matter and will bless the one who has had to live with disappointment.

Perhaps you do not have the problem of being childless. But you know what it is to say goodbye to that career you had in mind. Perhaps you have become reconciled to the fact you will not be getting married. Perhaps you have had to abandon hope of being healed. Maybe the move you longed for is not going to come. And could it be that you are locked into an unhappy marriage? Perhaps you agonize over that unanswered prayer. I myself finally conceded – only a few weeks before the retirement date came along after twenty-five years - that the revival I yearned and prayed for at Westminster Chapel was not coming after all. Hardly anybody could appreciate the pain this was for me. I preached a sermon called 'A Dream Deferred' - based on Habakkuk 3:17-18, to which the author refers in her own book:

> *Though the fig tree does not bud and there are no grapes on the vines, though the olive crop fails and the fields produce no food, though there are no sheep in the pen and no cattle in the stalls, yet I will rejoice in the Lord, I will be joyful in God my Saviour.*

If God were not sovereign, merciful and all-powerful, one would not be in agony over something they wanted so much. It is because God can do anything - but doesn't – that allows for the pain. And perhaps there will be readers who would not be the slightest bit bothered over what Malcolm and Nick went through. Few can appreciate Hannah's pain (1 Sam. 1:4-16) as well. But when you know God is able to step in, but chooses not to, it requires an immense faith and greater devotion to God.

We used to sing back in the hills of Kentucky as I grew up, 'Some day He'll make it plain to me'. In the meantime we adopt the spirit and stance of Job who proclaimed, 'Though he slay me, yet will I hope in him' (Job 13:15).

I commend this book to you in the hope that you too will bow to a Sovereign God whose ways are higher than ours but who works all things according to the counsel of his will.

R T Kendall
Key Largo, Florida
May 2005

1
WHY HAVE WE WRITTEN THIS BOOK?

That's a good question! Well firstly, it's not because we are qualified or better than anyone else. It is simply because we saw a need. When we first discovered that we had trouble conceiving I searched for a Christian book that would help. I found a handful and read them. They all had different points that helped us, but none scratched where we itched! One book was too scientific, another was helpful but didn't point us to the Lord, and one left us aching, numb and unable to find God in our situation. We wanted someone to be real with us, someone who had been where we were but who could also reassure us that God was here too! So this is simply our story, warts, struggles and all. If you pick this up hoping to find that everything is rosy and wonderful, you will find out that it isn't! This book will give you a taste of what we coped with during the years of infertility and how we managed. It will take you through the story of our miscarriage and the task of piecing our lives back together afterwards. It will take you to the places where we have met God in our heartache and have come out the other side stronger in Him. This book was not written on a whim. This book is our history.

Our story was written in the midst of our struggles and took an unexpected turn when we conceived naturally and then miscarried. You will see, as you read through our highs and our lows, that we have been honest and real. But hopefully you will also see that the Lord has carried us, made us stronger in Him, strengthened our marriage and has picked us up when we have fallen.

You need to understand that we are writing this book as born-again, spirit-filled Christians. If you can identify with our circumstances but do not have a relationship with the Lord, then we urge you to look into it. There's no pressure, but you've got nothing to lose. Quite the opposite – we assure you!

We pray that through the frailty of our words and the struggles of our experiences, this book will help you. You may be going through a similar situation to us or you could have a friend or family member that is facing the heartache of longing for or losing a baby.

As Christians we can sometimes be reluctant to share things with others. We have met many Christians over the years that were longing for a child, questioning and aching as we were. However, we only discovered these similarities when our friends eventually conceived or if the barriers came down and we finally felt able to share. Those couples that we shared with initially all have children now – some more than one or two! It would have been lovely to have known a couple that could have understood our situation fully and been there as we worked things through.

However, our pastors and their wives – Peter and Emma Cockrell and then Peter and Margaret Day – were a real blessing. They never had a 'go' at us for going over the same ground. I'm one of these people that used to feel that once you've had prayer for something then it's sorted. All those years of disappointment and broken dreams have shown me that you can be at a place of hurt, be prayed for and meet with

God, leave the room feeling positive, grateful for knowing Jesus, and in a matter of months, weeks or even days you can be right back to despair!

I was the only person that criticized me for needing repeated prayer and support. I was the only person to put me down. Neither of our pastors or their wives ever said, 'Oh no here she goes again' or 'Who pressed the repeat button this time?' They followed the example of Jesus and took us as we were! They didn't criticize. They supported, loved and prayed for us. God gave them the grace and patience to handle us in some very dark days. We were offered counselling by the hospital and GP numerous times. We never took it. God had provided us with people who loved Him and loved us. These friends would listen to us and point us to God. If you don't have support like this – pray for it!

As you read this book remember this is not what will happen if you face infertility or miscarriage. No one's story is the same. This is simply our story. This is the story of a young Christian couple. We are sharing things that we have discovered, and we pray that it will help others. We have been real and honest, which has not been easy. In writing this we have opened up our lives. It makes us vulnerable, as you will see our weaknesses and failings as well as the good moments. But a dear friend of ours once said to me, 'Vulnerable is a safe place to be when you are in the arms of God.'

This book does not mean that we have 'got ourselves sorted out'. We still do not have a child. We have lost a baby and to be really honest with you we are still learning. There have been times, even recently, where I have been struggling and have had to reread some of my own story to help me in the midst of the aching. Yes, we do still struggle, we still ache, we still cry and still have bad days. We don't have all the answers, but we do know a God who does!

We are praying that whether you read this in the heights or the depths, our story will encourage your heart and our Saviour will lift your gaze to Himself.

2
WHERE WE ARE COMING FROM

It was July 1993; I was just eighteen and going on a trip to the Lake District with our '18's plus' group from church. Little did I expect to meet a man who would change my life! This guy would love me and marry me despite my faults and unusual taste in socks! However, it was not love at first sight. In fact my first conversation alone with Malcolm went something like 'What's your problem – you don't like girls do you?'

Well to cut a long story short, seven months after that first meeting, Malcolm asked me if I would go out with him. I can't really describe how I felt except I couldn't stop smiling and every time the phone rang my heart missed a beat. With Malcolm in London and me living in Dunstable weekends became precious times together. In July of 1994 God opened up an opportunity for me to work at Spurgeon's College where Malcolm was already working. So I packed up and moved to London to start work as the college receptionist. In October Malcolm proposed. It was very romantic. Soft rain, peace, tranquillity, a light lunch – my ring was concealed in a Kinder Surprise egg as we sat together in Scratchwood Services on the M1. It has since been renamed the London Gateway but it will always be a special place for Malcolm and I!

9th September 1995 was our wedding day and it couldn't have been more perfect, with friends, family, work colleagues, and each other. It was truly wonderful. At the time we didn't think in depth about those words in the service about God ordaining marriage for people to have children.

We didn't take much notice of all the jokes like, 'When are you going to start a family,' and 'We thought we would buy you a cot for your wedding present.' After all, it was just fun. We already had three nephews and a niece and adored children. We had talked about having our own and how many we would want. Before we got married we had already agreed that we would have our children while we were still young so we could enjoy them for a longer time!

It was September 1996 when I came off the pill. Both of us were really excited about having children. We discussed names, started to get the child-care magazines, bought books on pregnancy and even talked about what colour to paint the baby's bedroom. We were both getting really excited. I clearly remember the first few months when my period came, dismissing it, telling myself that my body needed to adjust to coming off the pill. I reminded myself that not everyone gets pregnant in the first few months of trying. But after another couple of months we went to the doctors as we were beginning to wonder what was going on. The doctor told us not to worry about it until we had been trying for at least a full year and she assured us that we'd be back shortly to confirm a pregnancy! Confidently, we left the doctors thinking that by September I would be pregnant.

However this was just the beginning of a very dark valley. The valley of the shadow of infertility....

3
Coping with Infertility Treatments

Now this book does not deal with the different treatments you can get, nor will it tell you what is ethical or unethical. This is simply 'snippets' of things that we have experienced. For example, we found that many people would tell us what they thought when actually all we needed was someone to love us during a very difficult time. We needed people to help and encourage us when we felt isolated and alone in the medical system of infertility treatment.

I will never forget a dear man, in Lansdowne Church where we worshipped. He was the kind of guy that could fix anything and if he couldn't he knew someone who could! One

Sunday he stood at the front of the church with an overhead projector and laid his tools on it so that the screen simply had an outline of a hammer, screwdriver and other various 'manly' tools. He looked at the screen, turned back and said, 'My wife has been diagnosed with Breast Cancer. For the first time in my life there is something that I cannot fix and I can't do anything to try and remedy this situation.' This is exactly how I felt. There was nothing that I could do to become pregnant. I couldn't cheat, couldn't bribe, couldn't work harder – there was nothing, absolutely nothing, I could do. So began the long road of infertility investigations and treatments.

Infertility treatment must be amongst the most humiliating, degrading, embarrassing and emotional things that I have ever experienced. The first time I went to the hospital I lay in a room completely naked while I was prodded, poked and examined all over by a complete stranger. This stranger was very insensitive, he even asked Malcolm to leave the room while they did various things to me. It was a horrific experience for a young twenty-two-year-old. I was completely ashamed and humiliated. My first appointment left me so bitter, hurt and humiliated that I didn't get over it for years.

Even now the thought of that day makes me cringe. This left a lasting memory that meant every time I returned to the infertility department I felt ashamed, hurt and wished that I didn't have to be there. We had arrived at the hospital looking for answers and left with a label, 'INFERTILE'. Every appointment that we ever had at the hospital was preceded with weeks of fear and dread and was followed by days of relief – only because we had awhile before the next appointment. However, if another appointment loomed in the near future the fear would remain. Sometimes I had a constant dread of these appointments.

I remember one occasion where I was beginning a course of injections, blood tests and internal scans. A work colleague was going to drive me to the hospital for the first appointment. I got in the car and told her I was 'fine', at the end of our road I admitted that I didn't feel so good and by the time we had got round the corner I had thrown up in her treasured car!

Infertility treatment is a rollercoaster ride. My ride was made a whole lot worse by a consultant who I felt treated me like a slab of meat. It was as if I had no emotions to consider or questions that didn't need answering. On one occasion Malcolm and I asked him a basic question and he never even deigned to answer it. I couldn't bring myself to ask him again as I fought back the tears – I was so upset.

During one appointment the consultant had two students sitting in with him and he left the room to get something. While he was out of the room Malcolm asked the students not to follow the consultant's example in patient care! At one point, we were so unhappy with the consultant, we decided to go private. This would have been costly but we were prepared to do it (we'd have done anything!). However, the information arrived from the private hospital, only for us to discover that we would be under exactly the same consultant!

The other thing that I hated was the waiting room. It was full of hopelessness that oozed despair. Everyone knew why you were there. We all clutched the yellow document wallets we were provided with to keep our information in. We all sat wondering what the appointment would bring. We all desperately longed for the same end result but felt crushed by the process. This waiting room was strategically located so that all pregnant women had to pass it to get to the ultrasound and antenatal departments. You would watch these women pass by one after another while you would sit with all the other infertile couples and clutch your yellow document wallet in the 'waiting room of despair'.

During a series of treatments there was an appointment that I attended on my own. This was quite unusual, but as it was the middle of a run of treatments I was comfortable enough to go alone. I had been going daily for one thing and another and this day was to be a simple scan. Nothing major was to happen and, thankfully, I wasn't due to see the consultant! I remember lying there during the internal scan looking at the fertility nurse specialist. I prayed for positive words to come from her mouth. Malcolm and I had paid a whole chunk of money for this treatment (we had saved for it); we were both excited and I had been flicking through catalogues, reading pregnancy magazines – we were confident this was 'gonna work'!

I had been on such a high, I had dreamt of telling our parents, I had worked out roughly when our baby would be due, what sort of pram we would get, what time of year the dedication would be, boys' names, girls' names, middle names – my thoughts had been doing overtime! Malcolm had brought some baby 'padders' from the shops – we were ecstatic! We had no reason to doubt. We had been sold this treatment. We were confident that it would work. No one had said that it might not. We had heard nothing but positive comments on this treatment and these positive comments had been made with reference to our situation. The sales pitch was very convincing. This was the 'fix' we'd been waiting for! And now – well now I lay there, scan in progress, dreams in hand, nothing but joy lined up for us over the next year… but the nurse's face showed nothing!

'OK Mrs. Cameron. Sit yourself up.'

Wasn't she going to turn the monitor round so that I could see the very beginning of our dreams?

'The treatment hasn't been successful…'

I didn't hear what else she said. Someone had just ripped out my heart and stomped all over it. This was all a horrific nightmare. 'I must be dreaming – someone pinch me!' I was shown back to the side room to get dressed and wait for someone else to come and speak to me. I felt so alone, so helpless. I struggled to hold back the tears. I could hear the next person in the scanning room; the walls were not very thick!

'Oh yes, I see the fetus, oh hold on there's two…' Squeals of delight sounded from the new parents to be and then another announcement… 'How do you feel about triplets?'

Now my heart was not only broken, it was

in smithereens! I left the hospital choking back the tears and phoned Malcolm to pick me up. I couldn't see where I was walking as I sobbed my way along the pavement. My world had just fallen apart; my dreams lay in anguish; my hopes were more than dashed. When Malcolm picked me up I could hardly speak I was so distraught. He took me home to shower and change. He phoned my boss to say that I wouldn't be going back to work that day. I was in no state to cope. The tears were unrelenting. We'd lost our baby even before it had been created! 'Where was God? Why was this happening?' I was gutted!

So infertility treatment for me was a catalogue of hopes raised, intrusive procedures, various side effects, repeated disappointment and despair. I had pills, drugs, scans, injections and surgery. Countless men and women prodded and poked at me. At one time my arms and thighs were bruised for weeks because of the repeated blood tests and injections. I had really had enough! My emotions couldn't take it. Our marriage couldn't take it. My body couldn't take it, and it was doing my spiritual life no good at all.

It sounds from that last statement that the decision to finish with infertility treatment was an easy choice for us to make. Believe me it was one of the most difficult choices that we have ever had to make! If you are going to make a decision, like we did, to quit the medical treatments available, then you *must* agree as a couple, you *must* consult God on it and you *must* be happy with your decision. We actually stopped at one time for a year. Close friends had said that they could see we were struggling with the pressure of it all and they suggested that we had a break for awhile. However, after that year we began again and it wasn't till after the story of the failed treatment that I have just related that we made the decision to stop entirely.

There have been times when I have wondered about the decision we took. I've asked myself, 'If we had carried on would we have children by now?' There have been times when I've wished we had carried on, and then I remember what we went through. During one of those 'I wish we'd carried on' times a good friend asked me why we decided to stop. After I had given some reasons they looked at me and gently, lovingly, asked, 'Are you happy with your decision?' I simply replied, 'Yes.'

It was mid–2003 (some years after we had decided enough was enough). I went for a routine cervical smear, and during the procedure the nurse questioned me on what contraception we used.

'None', I replied – wondering why she asked when all this is on my notes!

Then came the full-blown lecture on going to a consultant for infertility treatment. She wouldn't let it drop despite my explanations and medical notes. She went on and on. I could happily have punched that nurse in the face. She had no idea what I had been through. My insides were seething and livid whilst my exterior was cool, calm and polite. I got home and phoned Malcolm. This woman, this complete stranger, had caused me to lose my peace Big Time!

Obviously infertility treatment did not work for us and no one should judge it on our story. Each person is different and copes differently. If this is a road you are on then your experiences may be the complete opposite of ours. I have simply recorded examples of what happened to us to help those who are also going through the pain and the ups and downs of such treatments.

If you are going through infertility treatment or about to embark on it these are just a few pointers that we discovered along the way (I hope these help you):

1. Talk together about it and how you feel. Always ensure that you both agree on whatever treatment you go for. Discuss what you feel is ethical or not ethical. This needs to be your decision as a couple.

How far will you go? This is not as easy as some Christians think. Some suggestions we were given took more research than the information that the hospital gave to us. Be honest, open and real with one another. This is easier said than done. We ended up having a 'How are you' session where we asked each other questions on how are you about kids, treatment, church, work, home, etc. This worked for us!

2. Be aware that in the UK not all NHS treatments are free. We found that the prescriptions and treatments required two separate amounts of money. Note that your GP will sometimes have to write a prescription for the drugs used on treatments at the hospital, and they are restricted by finances on how many times they will let you do it. Our GP only had to do this once. Initially he was reluctant, as it would cut into his 'budget'. When we went to see him we weren't sure whether he was going to prescribe or not. We don't understand all about it, we only know this by our experience, and the law may change anyway!

3. We were told, concerning some of the treatments we had that the success rate was high, after reading the material given to us we came to realize that a high success rate to the infertility medical profession is actually a low percentage rate. Don't do what we did and assume that the likelihood of a pregnancy not being achieved is remote – it is actually the other way round!

4. *Have another person or couple who can help you through it. However, you should both be happy about whom you talk to and you should try to ensure that you see them together. Having said that, in the early days I spent much time, one on one, with our pastor's wife. Sometimes it needs to be woman-to-woman and then man-to-man! When we began this long road of infertility treatment our pastor and his wife were a lifeline. We both knew that they were always there for us and they were never critical. They loved us when we needed it. After they left our new pastor was someone that we would talk to. He had a way of hearing from God and pointing us to God, just as our previous pastor and his wife had done before him. Our pastor's wife was a tower of strength for me in the early days. The first three or four years often found me in tears, aching or broken – each month the reminder came and the ache intensified. A sound godly person or couple will be vital for you. The times I have apologized for going back over the same ground and been told that it's OK!*

5. *Never get too excited too early – this is a toughie, but imagine doing what I did. I worked out the date of birth of our child and then nothing happened. Those nine months were a dark time for me. I wish I had never done it! I spent much of that time blaming God, questioning Him and being very bitter! This does not help you or your spouse!*

6. *If the fertility problem is with you then*

remember that the treatments affect your spouse too. They can feel helpless as they see all that you go through. They long for the same thing you do. Don't shut them out!

7. If the fertility problem is with your spouse then remember that they are not just coping with the emotions that you are, they are also handling the physical investigations, treatments and side effects. They will need your unconditional love with no pressure to achieve what they can't. Love them, build them up, be there for them and don't make them go through treatments if they aren't 100 per cent happy. Decide together what treatments you go for. Your spouse will feel an unspoken pressure to make you a parent; don't add to it!

8. Keep your focus on God – let this be a time where you grow rather than deteriorate. It would be so easy to turn your back on God and make hospital appointments, temperature taking, pill swallowing, timing of sexual relations, vitamin and mineral digesting more important than your relationship with God!

Here's food for thought to end this chapter – if you had children tomorrow, God's love for you will be just the same as it is now. No matter what, God will still be there. No matter how great things are or how bad things get – He is constant. Let your delight be in eternal things rather than the passing things!

4
COPING WITH PEOPLE PRESSURES

One of the reasons this book has been written is simply that we found there wasn't anyone that we could identify with in the nightmare of not being able to conceive. People around just didn't seem to understand. I realize that everyone who goes through this deals with it differently and won't have the same feelings as someone else. There is no wrong or right way. People's family, marriage, church, work, hospital and home situations are all different. God created us all differently. All the facts and figures about DNA tell us that we are different. Our characters are different too. So naturally we are all going to react differently!

I fell into the trap at one point of feeling that I was strange, not 'normal' (whatever normal is), that for some reason I was different in an odd kind of way. Well if you are struggling with 'not being normal', don't worry, you're as normal as they get! It is so easy for childless couples to feel abnormal. Everywhere you look there seems to be a pregnant woman, young babies and children. It can leave you feeling isolated, alone and that there is no one else experiencing what you are. Yes, we've felt like that too and that's why we saw a need for an honest book!

The one problem facing couples who are experiencing trouble conceiving is that it is such a taboo subject, such an emotional turmoil, such an embarrassing, even humiliating, topic, that no-one ever mentions it, especially in Christian circles. We found lots of couples that were struggling with an inability to conceive or from repeated miscarriages. They felt just the same things as we did yet we only discovered this as deepening friendships were made. The initial friendship didn't allow us to share our situation with each other. The problem this creates is that at first you begin to feel very alone. Everyone around you seems to be blooming or having babies! At one point everywhere I looked there were pregnant women, new babies, toddlers and children of all ages. It didn't matter what age the child was – it was just a visual reminder of a privilege that was denied to me. I couldn't turn to someone and say 'son', or 'daughter'. I didn't have a child to hold in my arms and caress, cuddle or just be with. Once, to encourage us, we were told of another couple that were struggling to conceive (no names were mentioned). The problem was that they fell pregnant fairly soon and the 'encouragement' that was meant turned into a bit of a 'slap in the face'. Even the encouragement that 'a miracle could happen for you too' didn't help when we were still trying with no success. It is easier said than done, but don't compare yourselves to others, it destroys rather than helps! For example, if you have a pregnant umarried woman at your church and you compare yourself with them it will eat away inside. 'Lord we have done everything right and this girl has been living in sin.' I guarantee that this approach will not only destroy you inside it will affect your relationship with God! Comparison is dangerous when it comes to infertility and it is best to steer well clear of it. Take my advice. I've done it, been there and had to sort out the consequences!

One of the hardest things that we found was how to react when others got pregnant. Yes, we have just discovered how comparison is dangerous, but on a practical note how do you cope when someone tells you that they are going to have a baby when you have tried for so long and nothing has happened? Malcolm will tell you that on every occasion I have said things like, 'We are so pleased for you', 'That's great news', 'When is it due?' – complete with a big smile on my face. When we are alone he has to pick up the pieces where I've wept furiously, declaring that it is *always* everyone else and *never* me.

There have been times when I have wept till the early hours of the morning, cried myself to sleep, walked the streets late at night in anger trying to release some of the pent-up emotions. And this is all because someone else has told me that they were expecting a baby.

We've had people tell us in various ways. Some have pulled us aside after church. Some tell us over the phone. Others have told us while they've been staying with us in our home. Some have come for a meal and told us during the middle of the first course. In fact there have been countless different ways! I have always preferred the short, sharp shock where within ten minutes of hearing their news I can cry. But sometimes I have had to suffer hours of putting on the happy smiley mask of 'we're thrilled for you!' Of course we were thrilled for them, but aching for us. I never ever wanted to hurt someone who had such good news so I never cried in front of them. I left that 'privilege' for Malcolm!

I often thought how hard it must have been for some people to tell us when they knew our situation. I learned to think of them and deal with myself later. It has never been easy and I praise God that pregnancies are nine months, because it usually gives me about six months to come to terms with the idea of a friend or colleague's new bundle of joy.

However, having said this, I do know that I didn't handle other people's pregnancies very well at all. I simply steered clear of that person. I now look at the way I was with some friends with regret in my heart, because I let my hurt get in the way of some very good friendships. Even steering clear of people and trying to mentally prepare myself for the big day didn't help. In fact nothing could get me ready to see a tiny baby when the inevitable did happen. Again the mask of smiles and joy took over. Later the ache caused tears to flow. Disappointment, failure and grief reared their ugly heads once again. So how to cope with this? I can't actually tell you because for me it is simply something that I have had to live through, to cry through and mask well. All I can say is next time someone tells you his or her good news, tell God how you feel and tell your spouse as well. The ache, hurt and disappointment are enough to cope with without adding resentment, anger, jealousy or disagreement to it!

With infertility being such a taboo subject in Christian circles it did present for us another problem: I have been to women's meetings or general conferences where I have plucked up the courage to go forward for prayer, making myself vulnerable, only to find the reaction of the prayer team unhelpful.

At one meeting women who were struggling with conceiving were invited forward for prayer. And on another occasion people living with disappointment were given the opportunity to receive prayer ministry. On both of these occasions the people praying for me just didn't know how to react or how to pray. I was hurting, broken and had plucked up courage to respond only to be disappointed because of a lack of understanding. Both times

I needed my husband or a friend to pray with me straight afterwards as the ache was so intense. Local churches need to be prepared to handle the taboo subjects in order to help the broken, confused and hurting in our society. We mustn't make rash comments. Before we pray we should wait on God and let the Holy Spirit prompt us about how to pray for someone. When broken people ask for prayer we need to pray sensitively. We need to be open to how that person is feeling and have sensitivity to the Holy Spirit.

One of the aches is how I was not able to see a child day in and day out. I love to see a baby's hands, ears and feet, to look at how intricately formed every little detail is – the lines on their fingers and their little knuckles. Everything is so perfect. Yet without your own family you miss the joy of seeing every new thing they experience from the first time they smile, talk or walk. There is no first time at crèche, Sunday school or the seaside. I felt and still do feel so deprived of these exciting moments. Life for me just wasn't complete.

If people haven't been through fertility struggles they can never feel the way you feel. They can't understand or even guess how you feel – no matter how hard they try. For us this was evident especially with close family. Our situation was completely foreign to them. We had to learn that it was hard for them as well. We couldn't expect them to know how we were feeling. Even if people have been through the same kind of situation they will feel differently to you. There may well be some similarities but other battles will differ immensely. The feelings of hope and then sheer desperation can be hard for other people to grasp. We found that the hardest people to talk to about our infertility struggles were close family. It was easier for us to share with people who were close friends but not related. Years later we discovered how hard it had been for our parents who longed to know what was happening, but couldn't ask us. My mum said to me that there were times that she wanted to know but was reluctant to ask because she didn't want to upset me. Both sets of parents did just what we needed them to do. They were simply there for us if we needed them. They were 'normal' with us in a very painful time. It was hard for them and we never really grasped that till some years had passed.

So we have seen that we are all different and everybody who goes through the struggles of childlessness deals with it and experiences it differently. So how do we cope when well-meaning comments come our way that actually end up being very unhelpful?

Here are some of the comments Malcolm and I have had to handle:

'So when are you two going to have children?'

'When are you going to start a family?'

'I've got some baby clothes and things do you want them?'

On one occasion we were even told that in some cultures it was legal for a man to divorce his wife if she was infertile. You can imagine how helpful that was! Comments like these can leave you deeply hurt. They can turn you from being content and happy with your current situation to upset and desperate all over again. We learnt that it doesn't take a lot to make the rollercoaster head downwards; even the tiniest of 'harmless' comments can do it! There is no set way to handle these situations, but Malcolm and I have both found that you need to bear in mind that this person has no idea what you are going through. They are probably just joking, or having fun. Perhaps they don't necessarily want a serious reply and are just unsure about what to say to you. This is one place where you can have a valuable and practical lesson on how to be gracious!

I remember one student at the college who, whenever I saw him or spoke to him on the phone, would ask 'When are we going to hear the pitter patter of tiny feet?' This went on for years and eventually one day he said that he did not understand why we didn't want to have children. He and his wife loved their kids so much and it was the best thing that had ever happened to them. I asked the Lord to give me grace and I looked him in the eyes. Simply and calmly I said, 'If Malcolm and I are to have children that really will be down to God not us.'

I could have said lots of things, but I feel that they would only have caused him to walk away feeling hurt. Instead he walked away thinking through my reply and coming to his own conclusions. Grace is vital when replying to difficult comments. If you're not sure what to say, then take a deep breath and ask the Lord to give you the words to say. I have read books where people who could not have children would work out what to say to certain comments for example, if someone said, 'When are you going to start a family?' they would reply 'We're already a family – we have been since the day we got married.' This is fine, but if you say it slightly snappy or abrupt it could crush the person who was asking a basic question. There are no set answers – you need to pray for grace, love and wisdom.

As Christians, let us talk to one another how we would want to be talked to. Just because you are going through a difficult situation doesn't mean to say that you have the right to make everyone else suffer. A lot of people guessed with us that we couldn't conceive, others asked, and others only found out when we became pregnant and miscarried. We never made announcements about it and we never told people that we weren't comfortable with. We do know that others who knew did tell other people (you know the Christian gossip – oops I mean prayer network!!). We didn't mind so much after six or seven years of trying, but in the initial years we limited whom we told. We were still trying to come to terms with it ourselves without dealing with other people's feelings as well!

There was another time when we gave some hospitality to a dear man of God. He stayed in our home for a week and shared with us about how he had prayed for some mutual friends who had had trouble conceiving. Malcolm and I looked at one other, but didn't say anything. Hastily we changed the conversation. The next day Malcolm spoke to him quietly, bloke-to-bloke, just to let him know about our own situation. We had discussed telling him our story before then but had decided that we didn't really know him that well. But now I can emphatically say that as a couple, Malcolm and I have grown to really respect this man as a faithful and prayerful man of God. He stayed with us again when I was pregnant before the miscarriage and shared in our joy at that time. Imagine though if we had dealt with the initial conversation in a different way. What would have happened if Malcolm had immediately jumped in with the fact that we couldn't conceive and that I had been through various procedures? I would have been highly embarrassed, as would he. It could have left this man feeling very uncomfortable. Perhaps he would never have stayed with us again. I praise God that Malcolm handled this situation so tactfully. So don't feel that you have to respond to a comment or conversation immediately. Give yourselves a chance to talk as a couple first if needed.

One thing that we have really had to battle with is people close to us who have tried to 'encourage' us by saying that if we had a child or children we wouldn't be able to do the work with the young people in the church. This was and still is a toughie because to a certain point it could be true. We don't know for certain because we haven't got children, but the hurt we felt and the void ache sometimes left us wishing that God would give us a different job in the church that could be done if we had children. It's quite hard to grasp but it made us almost resent God's call on our lives. We knew that God wanted us to be working with the under-16s at church, but if it meant that we were called to remain childless then that was a different matter. We worked through this one together. It was a long hard battle. Sometimes when people try to encourage others the repercussions can actually be negative! God has helped us with this to the extent that we are able to pray, 'Whatever Lord.' We trust Him. We have a simple unexplainable trust for our calling, ministry with young people and for whether or not we ever become parents!

We were told several times that our infertility must be God punishing us for something. I remember trying to work out what it was that I had done so wrong to deserve this terrible punishment. I couldn't think of anything and so I racked my brains to think of every sin ever committed. I tried to work out which one

I was being punished for. I wanted to find out which sin it was so that I could ask forgiveness and the punishment would stop. This probably sounds ridiculous but I was unsure how else to handle being told it was a punishment. A friend eventually pointed out to me that Jesus took our punishment *completely* on the cross. I knew this, but having more than one person tell you that it was a punishment, to your face, will cause you to ask some serious questions! I know that sometimes God does discipline us, but situations like this should not cause us to ask 'Why?' but to ask, 'What is the purpose?' 'What is God teaching me?' 'To what end, Lord?' God has His purposes for the things that we go through. Sometimes we see them and sometimes we don't! We need to ensure that we do not allow our circumstances to change how we view the character of God. For example, when I was told that this was a punishment it conjured up a picture of God as a tyrant with a big stick rather than a loving, merciful and faithful heavenly Father. We need to have a biblical view of God whatever we face in life.

This chapter could go on and on in light of the number of unhelpful things that have been said to us. It's so hard to handle others, comments and advice, especially when it comes with a lack of understanding. On a handful of occasions we have been told that we will have a child – sometimes even given dates, names or the sex of the baby. This sounds strange but each time it happened it was very hard. It never once brought encouragement. For me it brought a fear of allowing my hopes to be raised, only to be crushed again. Once when this happened it left me really shaky, tearful and unsure what to do with what had been shared with me. It had caught me completely off guard! I guess that when these things are said we must make sure that it doesn't take our focus off God. We must entrust Him with whether or not what has been shared will happen or when it will happen. The other danger in people pressures is misused or misquoted verses of Scripture, for example, Matthew 6:33, 'But seek first his Kingdom and his righteousness, and all these things will be given to you as well.' I was told in light of this verse that our infertility was down to the fact that Malcolm and I were not seeking God first and if we did that we would conceive! We need to keep a biblical view of the character of God as we mentioned earlier. God does not bribe us to seek Him first, to follow Him. The other Scripture that I misinterpreted was about children being a reward from God.

This is in Psalm 127. But as we will see in the chapter on examples from Scripture later on, children are in fact a gift and God is the One who enables conception to happen.

When it comes to handling people's comments, work out whether what they are saying is in line with what God is saying. When unhelpful things are said give them over to God, don't let them fester. I know that I've let unhelpful things overtake my thoughts – it can be crushing! Talk to God, talk to your spouse or if necessary talk to someone that you both trust whose theology is firmly grounded in Scripture. We've needed this on several occasions. Our pastors have always been so helpful in answering our questions and pointing us to God.

You must also, where necessary, forgive the person who has hurt you. Don't let something that was said ruin your relationship with them! I did a lot of forgiving with support from two friends. It was costly. It took time. It took tears but it brought closure on hurts, some of which had been open, sore and throbbing for years. In a room with two friends praying and supporting me I forgave these people in my heart and before the Lord. Sometimes we need to do this and maybe other times we do actually need to talk to the person face to face, but this MUST be done with the right attitude, as they may not realize that they have hurt you. The list of unhelpful things that people have said to us is lengthy and we have only shared a handful as examples. We are still learning to constantly be on our guard, to weigh with Scripture what is said, to guard our responses and to guard our thoughts as well – it's not easy and we are definitely still learning!

So, what can we say about the pressure to produce a child or grandchild, niece or nephew? Nothing was ever really said to us about this, but we did feel a pressure from family. Other members of the family were producing children left, right and centre. Meanwhile we remained as just Malcolm and Nick! When we decided to not go through any more hospital treatment there were questions from various quarters. The important thing is that you as a couple are happy and confident with decisions you make and that no matter what, you put God first and foremost. If you ensure that God is the centre of your marriage you cannot go wrong. When asked, we told people that we were leaving it firmly in the hands of our sovereign God and if they really wanted us to have a child they could take it up with Him directly. It seems a simple thing to say and again you need to ensure that it is said with grace and not abruptly, but the pressure that it removed, especially from me, was staggering!

I know it's not easy when you long to introduce your parents to their new grandchild and it just doesn't seem to happen. I know the frustration of going to a family 'do' and being the only one without kids. It's not easy and it doesn't get easier, but if you tackle each struggle together as a couple and talk it through, go to the Lord and tell Him exactly how you feel, then your marriage will grow stronger and you won't become consumed with the situation. Be honest with God and where necessary find someone outside of the marriage, outside of the family who can be independent and listen, as well as support you in prayer. We would choose to talk to someone that we were both comfortable with, who was faithful and who has a close relationship with the Lord. When we have shared with someone who hears from the Lord crucial areas have been dealt with in our lives. An example of this is when we were with our pastor and his wife and they were praying for us – mid-prayer our pastor stopped and looked at me, I remember clearly he said, 'I need to ask you about this.' God had shown him something that was a huge battle for me and although Malcolm knew about it we had never spoken about it. Through this man being obedient to what God had revealed to him we were able to talk and they were able to advise and pray. That day I left their home with lightness in my spirit. The heaviness had been lifted. This is just one example, but it has happened time and time again for both Malcolm and I. God has shown people what to ask us, how to pray and even given us words from the Lord that have been spot-on!

While someone was praying for me one day I had a picture as they were praying, then to my amazement they prayed the same picture that I was seeing even to a small detail. If it had happened the other way round and I prayed it and they were seeing it, I would have doubted, but because they prayed it and I had already seen it there was no doubt in my mind! We need to trust God. He knows what is best. We know this and believe this and yet we panic that He will bring things to light that we don't want dealing with! I am guilty of that. I had a habit of putting pressures on myself. Some of these thoughts that I had and pressures that I put on myself were very serious and knotted me up inside big time. I can't explain it all; I guess

I was mentally and emotionally self-harming. I would constantly put myself down. It was through trusted fellow believers who did not know what I was putting myself through that God came and broke those knots.

I think the most valuable lesson that I learnt towards the end of 2003 was that we do need to be honest with God. As a child I saw people week by week who responded to the question 'How are you?' by saying, 'Fine thanks – how are you?' This I learnt was a good Christian answer. I learnt that the immediate answer to 'How are you?' was 'Fine.'

There were weeks for me where I was broken by infertility, where my hopes had been raised and then crushed, and then I would walk into church and be asked how I was. Even when it was my closest of friends I would just say, 'Fine.'

We have to learn that this is lying and therefore a sin. We are family – the Body of Christ – and we need to learn to be honest with one another. I am not saying that when people ask you that you should blurt out everything. You need to share sensitively. But rather than 'fine' maybe just say that you are struggling a bit or that you would value their prayers. You don't need to tell them what you are struggling with, but you don't need to fob people off with an answer that isn't true either! I am still learning to do this! However, we also do this with God when we pray. We are so busy sometimes ensuring that we have prayed for everyone on our list and all the things in the diary that we actually forget to tell God how we are feeling! I am still learning this as well!

So let me try and summarize:

- *We're all different – there is no right or wrong way to cope.*

- *Just because you are hurting don't hurt others.*

- *Don't reply hastily – sometimes talk as a couple before you share.*

- *Don't be afraid to pray and ask for grace for a moment.*

- *Ensure God is the centre of your marriage.*

- *No matter what you face make sure you keep a biblical view of the character of God.*

- *Be honest with God especially about how you are feeling.*

- *Find a person or couple that will support you and pray with you and for you. Prayer is about listening to God as well and they should do this too.*

- *Be honest with fellow Christians – but be sensitive!*

It's OK to Cry

5

COPING WITH EMOTIONS

I have found that that there are times when I
am fine and can talk quite openly with folks. But
there are other times when I can't talk about the
whole children issue at all. This results in me
being quite tearful and even one silly comment
or question could send me into floods of tears.
Malcolm asked once why it was at one point
in the day I could be fine and then later in the
same day I could start crying for no apparent
reason at all. I had to tell Malcolm that I didn't
understand myself and I still don't!

It was almost three years into our 'infertility
years' when someone challenged me about
showing self-control. I had been going through

a bad couple of months with one or two highs and then lots of *very* deep lows. I had cried myself to sleep most nights and had been in tears often. I thought this comment was very insensitive, but after thinking about what they had said I thought that maybe I should try and exercise self-control in my emotional life. Needless to say it didn't work! Well, perhaps it did for a few months or so. I kept well away from the subject of children, smiling sweetly and refusing to let my emotions get control over me. I was a bit like a fizzy-drinks bottle being turned up and down. I refused to let anyone in to those innermost thoughts and feelings, including Malcolm. I *was* exercising self-control and my emotions were not going to be touched. The problem is, eventually someone undoes that bottle lid and then what happens! Whoosh! That kind of happened to me. The force of all the emotion, hurt, heartache and grief sent the lid flying and my tears flowed for a long time and with much anguish.

My theory, then, is that it is OK to cry. Don't tie yourself up in knots trying to be in control. Although some self-control is required, sometimes it will be inappropriate. I remember one evening where Malcolm and I were on our knees beseeching the Lord for children. We wept together before the Lord and it did us both good. It drew us together and we both felt that it was almost as though Jesus was weeping with us and feeling our pain. But I am not saying that you can burst into tears for the sake of it. There still needs to be an element of self-control.

Let me give you a personal example from the middle of 2003. I had been upset by something in the sermon one Sunday night. (I had taken something that was said the wrong way and applied it incorrectly to our situation on childlessness.) I knew that I needed to sort it before I went home, but I could have just wept. I was hurting inside. After the service the preacher came up to me and asked me if I was OK. I admitted that I was struggling over something that had been said. So we went aside and talked. Yes, I cried, but we sorted out the misunderstanding and God ministered to the area in which I was hurting. Yes, I was upset. Yes, I needed to sort the issue, but rather than blowing a gasket I was able to talk and showed self-control. Now it did help that God had prompted the preacher to ask me if I was OK. It's much harder for me to initiate the conversation in a situation like that!

There does come a point when you cannot

help but cry. (I've been there many, many times.) This is OK You should not feel condemned, because you are human and have feelings. No matter how good our theology, how strong our relationship with God – we all have feelings and at times we need to let them out rather than suppress them! If something particular has happened it is good for us to cry and to let the emotion out; but there comes a point when God meets us in those tears.

I cried a *lot* when the hospital stopped a cycle of treatment because it wasn't working. I cried with Malcolm. I cried on the phone talking to my pastor's wife. I cried in the shower. I cried as I got dressed and I cried as I prayed. I didn't cry as I listened to a tape of a sermon. I had put my focus back onto God and not the disappointment of that truly horrible day. We've all read Psalms where the writer has been in the 'depths of despair'. As the Psalm goes on, though, they reflect on how good God is, and what He has done. They end up singing a song of praise and exaltation of the Lord our God. I have put a personal example of this elsewhere in this book, 'Nick's Prayer After the Miscarriage'. It is very personal and isn't written like the Psalmist, but it came from my heart in a desperate hour. We will be looking later at the medicine of praise and prayer, so if emotions are one area you find hard to handle this will be a key chapter for you!

Jesus showed His emotions in different ways by His love for the sick, the young and the old – in fact for everyone. Jesus had a love for children, He wept when Lazarus died. He got angry with the merchants in the temple, and I am positive that He showed emotion when He preached and taught. It was His Father that He spoke about and how essential it was for people to be right with God. *Yes*, I'm sure that *He* would have showed emotion! He knew joy, He wept. He felt pain, anger and sorrow. So I wonder why I struggle so often with showing emotions when our chief example for Christian living showed such obvious emotion and with such passion?

Let's have a quick look at Job. OK, so God had blessed this man and he had children but gosh did he lose *everything* (including his children). Have a quick read in Job 1 to see. The verse that hits me time and time again when I read the book of Job is verse 22 – 'Job did not sin by charging God with wrongdoing.' So often when life deals us a tough situation we blame God. I know that I have experienced that. I have been angry, but look at Job. He must have cried when his children died. In fact he displayed a sign of deep grief in Job 1:20 when he tore his robe and shaved his head. He showed emotion, but he never blamed God. In fact Job did the opposite. After showing his emotion and displaying his grief we are told in Scripture that he fell to the ground in worship. He was not bitter towards God. Wow, what an example to us!

Proverbs 13:12 says, 'Hope deferred makes the heart sick'. After awhile desperation and disappointment can overwhelm us. They make our hearts sick with anguish. We need to learn to give this to Jesus. He came to bind up the broken-hearted and I know now what it is to have a broken heart. I didn't know before this started. I have felt the pain around my whole being and needed people that I have trusted to pray with, or for me. I also know what it is for God to meet me and touch my heart and make it whole again. A quote from Warren Wiersbe that I love is, 'God can heal the broken-hearted – if all the pieces are given to Him.' It's hard when one of those pieces is so precious, so longed for. But to give your children to God even prior to Him creating them will only bring long-term peace and a trust that is unquestioning! It is so hard to give something away even before you've received it. It takes faith, hope and maturity.

Maybe you have read this and you are in the midst of brokenness and hurt. I wish that I could be in the room with you to encourage you, but I know that Father God is right there with you. So if you are battling with sorrow, pain and a broken heart, take a moment out and tell God how you are feeling, allow Him to minister His grace and give Him every part of your broken heart. You can't expect Him to repair it if you are clinging on to a piece that you simply refuse to let go of. When the days are dark and you just want to cry, do it – but then take time and get your focus on God. Maybe try what I did and write a prayer, tell God how you are feeling. You may find that this becomes a way for healing to come and for your spouse to share in how you feel. Take courage my friend – your heavenly Father knows!

6
To Hug and to Hold

When we made our marriage vows it was a beautiful day. We knew God's hand was upon us and He set a seal upon our wedding day. It is very easy to stand in a church packed with friends and family – smiles all round, feeling so special – and speak words of commitment and promise – for better for worse, etc. However, it is a different thing to live it! What about when the 'worse' does happen? We stood there in a church hearing about marriage being a base for family life, having children and so on. We never even dreamt that this was the start of a marriage full of fun, laughter and happy times hand in hand with a long journey full of heartache and disappointment for us.

To begin with neither of us quite knew how to talk about it. We had jointly decided that I should come off of the pill. We were so excited, and after a few months of not conceiving dismissed it along the lines of sometimes it takes longer than you think. I will never forget our first appointment at the hospital. I was prodded, poked, examined and to my horror watched the medical personnel write 'infertile' on my file. We went in hoping for answers and left with a label! The early days saw me unable to voice to Malcolm how I felt, unable to confide in him. I saw him desperately wanting to help but unsure of how to. For a time the realization of infertility and the pain of repeated disappointment created a communication breakdown where we just did not talk about 'it'. However, after years of ups and downs this did eventually lead to a strengthening of communication and of our marriage. It took a long time though. It wasn't an overnight thing! I remember saying to Malcolm, 'If our marriage can withstand this it will withstand anything.'

In that time when communication was not good I didn't talk to Malcolm about how I felt. I was only young. I wasn't sure if I should, as well as that I wasn't sure how I felt, and the other reason was that I just couldn't!

We did find a way around this, however. We found a way for me to communicate about it to a certain degree without saying anything hard. Malcolm would ask me what was wrong and I would simply reply, 'just stuff'. The word stuff was our code word for this situation. It was a word that I could say to him without becoming a sobbing wreck! It was hard, the more I didn't talk about it the worse I felt. There were one or two that I would confide in, but I was a 'good Christian', anytime someone asked me how I was, I simply gave that good Christian answer, 'Fine!' I was a broken person with a mask of 'everything is OK'. Inside my heart was broken and I was gutted, disappointed and hurting. Outside I was doing and saying all the right things.

It has taken years for me to have the mask removed and be able to tell someone how I really am. God challenged me on why I was not honest even with Him. He already knew how I felt but I didn't tell Him. Malcolm was guessing how I felt without me saying anything. It took a long time to learn and a lot of practice but we did learn to talk together, to be open and to even pray about it together. We wept together. We shared hope together. We tasted disappointment together, but whatever came we dealt with it together. Even when the miscarriage happened we experienced it together, and then worked out our grief together and during the week after it, when each hour was different, we shared regularly, each day, how we were feeling!

When we got married the verse in Ecclesiastes 4:12 was 'our text'. The second part of it reads, 'A cord of three strands is not quickly [or easily] broken.' It was so special to us that we had it engraved on the inside of our wedding rings. This has been the key for us. It is not that we are two perfect people with a perfect marriage, rather it is that we are two Christian people working out our salvation with fear and trembling. We are working out our marriage, keeping God as number one, encouraging each other in the Word and in worship, and building one another up. We never put each other down to anyone and we always support one another no matter what!

God is the centre of our marriage! Does this mean that our marriage isn't in need of some work? No. We still have to guarantee that we have at least one night a week that is 'ours'. We go out on a 'date' regularly. We take time to go away just the two of us for weekends. We still have the day-to-day things to do. Finances need to be juggled, DIY has to be done (eek), housework, our jobs, youth work at the church – the list is endless! We make mistakes but we make them together and so we learn from them together.

We pray for each other so we see the answers together! We have learnt to handle anger and frustration together and then learnt to forgive one another. Before we were married Malcolm's dad gave us a text from Ephesians 4:26-27, 'Do not let the sun go down while you are still angry, and do not give the devil a foothold.' In light of this we learnt to ensure that disagreements, hurt or anger were dealt with before either of us went to sleep at night. On one occasion we sat till the early hours sorting out a disagreement. The next day I loved Malcolm more than ever. The hurt of the night before was dealt with, forgiven and forgotten, and this was a new day with a new start! Admittedly Malcolm and I do not often disagree or argue – we tried it, are rubbish at it, so we don't bother doing it! But there are odd times when we have disagreed and as a result we have had to sort things out!

So our relationship together is vital, but

under the title of this chapter comes a very sticky wicket that I have struggled with many times! I have battled time and time again with the 'if you had only married someone else' syndrome. I need to explain at this point that our infertility lies firmly with me, Nick. Malcolm is OK and has no problems! I battled with this for years. If Malcolm had chosen someone else to marry he would be a dad by now and his parents would be grandparents. I used to apologize to Malcolm all the time that I could not give him a child. I was hurting Malcolm by listening to the lies that the enemy was whispering and then believing them.

So you ask, when did this come to a crunch – it was around the end of August 2003 and a Sunday night, after the evening service. I was sitting, chatting to our pastor about something completely unrelated. It had been concerning me over recent days in my walk with the Lord and my pastor asked if he could pray about it. No problem. After he had finished praying about this other situation he was convicted by the Holy Spirit to pray about us having kids. (Malcolm was there praying with us too.) God came and released a lot of things that I had been struggling with and afterwards I turned to Malcolm and apologized that I hadn't been able to make him a dad.

Our pastor stepped in and spoke with authority. He was very clear and told me that this was a lie that I should not believe. Malcolm then confirmed that he did not marry me because of the children he hoped we'd have. He'd married me because he loved me!

This story highlights vital areas for us. Firstly: tell each other often that we love one another and not apportion blame for infertility. OK, so the problem does lie with me, but it's hardly going to help if Malcolm points that out and says it's all my fault. Secondly: Christian couples need support. One thing Malcolm and I will openly admit is that we are not good at praying together, especially over the children issue. There have been times where we have been unable to pray. Then there has been a timely conversation or someone has insightfully prayed for us. We have not gone round telling people that we have needed their support. God has shown us the right people at the right time. Initially this was our pastor and his wife who were there for us. They always had an open door. The pastor's wife came with me for hospital appointments when Malcolm couldn't, and they would both point us to the Lord in the bleakness of the barren lows! Our next pastor, along with his wife, were key, especially during the pregnancy and miscarriage.

Of course the other thing that you do have to face as people find out is unhelpful comments and even unhelpful suggestions or advice which we have covered elsewhere, but as far as your marriage goes, do not let bitterness enter your life in any shape or form. It will only do you and your marriage harm.

I realize that I have written this about marriage from our experience and that the problem is with me. I have tried to imagine what it must be like if the problem actually is with your man! Obviously this isn't easy to do, but in some ways I can see this as being tougher! Firstly, we need to acknowledge that it says clearly in Scripture that the man is the head of the household. This is not so that he can lord it over his wife, but it is so that he can bring a godly covering. If a man suffers with infertility problems I can imagine how that would make him feel useless or worthless. Although this is the same with women, it is probably far harder for a man to cope with. It is a very destructive feeling.

My fear for a wife, whose husband is infertile, is the temptation to take action into her own hands. You can be so desperate for a child that this could be a genuine thought. I would say to you that it is not worth it – hold on to your marriage, your husband and obey God. Couples never ever put your spouse down. This is something that I am so glad never happened with me. Malcolm not once pointed the finger at me, blamed me or made me feel worthless. I'm not just talking about putting your spouse down to their face. Malcolm and I agreed before we were married that we would never put each other down to anyone else. If we had a problem with something that the other had done we agreed to tell one another straight out. This has stood us in good stead, but it has also been taken a step further. If either of us is in the same room when someone is putting our other half down then we counteract this with a positive approach and truth. Malcolm is very hot on this and on occasions where I have been criticized over things, he will come straight out with truth and positive words. Sorry for the digression, but it was an important one. Guys who are struggling with infertility – I would strongly recommend you to find a godly guy that you trust to share with and pray with. You will need the support of a fellow bloke who can identify with you and support you, but whatever you do, don't cut your wife out – talk to her!

Let's summarize:

• *Love one another.*

• *Try and share with one another (this isn't easy). A tip for this that we found worked is a 'How do you feel' session. This is when you sit down together alone and ask lots of 'How do you feel' questions: i.e. How do you feel about church, home, work, us, having kids... It can be anything and everything and it doesn't need to be long or intense, we found it very helpful! Although, you must both want to do this question and answer session at the same time. It mustn't be forced! I know that we have mentioned feelings a lot in this chapter and in this book. They are so important and you really do need to share them with one another or it will only cause problems. Feelings are very important. Don't disregard how you or your spouse feels!*

• *Hug one another often.*

• *Support one another.*

• *Never put your spouse down (especially to other people). Only build them up.*

• *Pray for one another.*

• *Point each other to God especially on the tough days.*

And one last thing for this chapter…

- *Sex! Enjoy one another. Do not let your longing for sexual intercourse to result in conception rob you from delighting in one another. This is key. Let me repeat that another way. Don't let your longing for a child rob you of enjoying each other. Sex is a beautiful gift from God, not a bargaining tool, a reward for a partner or a stress. It is a gift from God for man and wife to enjoy. Don't let this area become a place that causes hurt or a thing that must be done on this day or that. Just enjoy it!*

I praise God for my husband – I can honestly say that God hand-picked him for me, and although the years since we first got married have been the toughest, they have also been the best!

7

MAN TO MAN: A NOTE FROM MALCOLM

This is a strange thing for me to do – Nick asked me if I would write a chapter of this book. At first I didn't want to, but the more I thought about it the more I realized that I needed to write about what Nick and I have been through over these last years and how that has affected me as the man, the husband.

As you will already know my name is Malcolm and I have been married to Nick since the 9th September 1995 – an amazing day! I would have to say that since we've been married these have been the best years in my life, and, as Nick has said, probably the hardest as well.

I was brought up in a Christian home and had an amazing childhood with my parents being missionaries with a well-known Christian organization. I got to experience lots of different things and go to a variety of different countries. Some people would say I had a very good childhood with varied opportunities all the time. When you look closer, though, what really matters is my grounding in Christ from my earliest days. So what has that got to do with what has happened to us over these years where we have struggled so much? Well, without the love, support and example that my mum and dad showed, I'm not sure I could have ever dreamt of writing this chapter, let alone cope with all that life has thrown at us. During my teens I spent most of the time away from the Lord and getting messed up with smoking, drinking, etc. God was not important to me at all. At the age of twenty-one I was challenged to take a closer look at my walk with God. It felt that I met with Jesus for the very first time even though I had become a Christian almost ten years earlier; it was only now that knowing Jesus was having an effect.

The difficult times since Nick and I were married have made my teenage life look like a walk in the park. These last years have tested my faith and my love for Nick in ways that I can't really express. My hope is that what I am sharing in these few words will encourage you to look to God and share your heart and feelings with your wife and, where necessary, other people that you can trust. I just want to share some of the highs and lows over these years and how God has become my passion and I hope will become yours.

Since we've been married I have gone through a range of emotions from excitement, pain, hurt, envy, fear, anger, loneliness, love, and many, many, more! Almost any emotion you can think of – all of them have been around at some time or another.

Just after we were married we started talking more seriously about having children and a mix of fear and excitement grew each time we talked about it, along with the endless lists of names that we came up with! When we realized that things weren't quite what we expected, the excitement began to turn to fear of the unknown. I didn't know what to say to Nick. There were many times we would look at each other and not know what to say. I can remember spending many hours trying to work out what Nick was feeling and then opening my mouth and putting both feet in it!

Over time I began to learn that I didn't always need to say something. I learnt the importance of hugs and cuddles!

Nick has already said about the 'How are you doing' times that we had. Well to be honest at first I hated it. I didn't like to be asked about how I felt. I had spent years not telling anyone. I was strong and knew how I was supposed to react to different situations. After all I was part of the leadership of the church. I worked with the young people. I was responsible for audio. I was a deacon, a trustee and people looked to me to solve problems.

In time the 'How are you' chats became really helpful. They weren't too long or pressured and enabled me to find out how Nick was feeling, at the same time as sharing how I felt. They were never regular or long, but they were key times. In fact they only lasted a couple of minutes, but a lot was said in that few minutes. Words that we both needed to say or hear!

I would really encourage you to be real with who you are. You are human and it's all right to be vulnerable. You don't always have to have an answer, you don't always have to be strong and it's OK to cry.

Learn to talk about how you feel. This sounds easy but it has taken me years to realize this. Nick often asked me, 'How are you doing?' My instant answer would be, 'Fine.'

As the husband there is so much to learn about your wife! I never knew about the menstrual cycle, the way in which hormones change and how this makes your wife feel. No one ever talked about it. This is where I've felt out of my depth, even lonely, and on some occasions angry or frustrated with myself. I've also felt angry and frustrated with Nick and definitely with God. The key to sorting out these feelings is getting your focus on God. I would encourage you to keep close to Him, find people around you who you can talk and pray with. Our pastors, and their wives, have been a constant support and blessing to us. They have always pointed us to God. I have trusted both of these men and have been able to share honestly with them. They have given me good advice and understood me even in the most desperate of situations. One of these guys was so helpful after the miscarriage. I spent some time with him and as I shared briefly he just looked at me and said, 'I know.' These two simple words helped so much. I had a fellow man that could identify with me in that awful time. Our present pastor was my best man and I was his. We have been good friends for years before he became my pastor as well as my friend. I have really valued that friendship through the years of infertility and during the miscarriage.

A question that you may be asking, which I know I have asked so many times, is 'What do I do?' So what do you do when your wife says, 'If only you had married someone else', or 'I'm useless, how can you say you love me', or 'I'm ugly and what have I done wrong?' How do you cope with such questions when each one hurts to the core of your being? You keep on asking, 'What do I do? What do you want me to say?' All I could do was to love Nick and tell her that I loved her. I reminded her that I chose her and that she is beautiful. The frustration for me of not being able to do anything, especially during appointments at the infertility clinic, was overwhelming. The most difficult thing was to see my wife go through traumatic tests. I hated the thought of Nick's internal examinations. All I could do was watch and pick up the pieces afterwards! I felt helpless, lost and couldn't do a thing.

My challenge to you as you read this is how much do you love your wife? What are you prepared to go through? What is your desire for the rest of your life? Why did you marry her? Did you marry her because you loved her or because you wanted to have children with her? If you can honestly answer these questions knowing that you love your wife more than anything else in the world, well you will make it through. I know that this sounds really harsh but you need to love your wife in order to make it through. You need to love her in the best and the worst of times.

I would encourage you, as a man, to seek God, to spend time with God and allow the presence of the Holy Spirit to overwhelm your life. To be the husband that you need to be you should spend time in the presence of the Almighty God. Then, each time you need to be strong for your wife you will be more equipped and able to draw on the resources that are bountifully available from God.

Be warned and be prepared, as you will be blamed for almost anything. Sometimes the husband just has to take it on the chin! You will have to go through huge changes in emotions over the days and months. Each month I can remember differences in how I felt and how Nick felt. Each month was hard for Nick, but also hard for me. I still had to cope with disappointment, frustration, sadness, and, on some occasions, grief.

I've rambled on long enough so I'll try to summarize.

As the husband you too will have to deal with emotions, your's and your wife's!

Be as real and honest as you can with each other.

Remember to talk to each other, spend time together and alone!

Make Jesus the centre of your life and your marriage.

Read the rest of this book, as you will hopefully find our story helpful. You may be able to identify with us so that you don't feel so alone or isolated.

Just one last thought, always build each other up and look to God, take each day as it comes.

Note for the guys from Nick:

Sorry to butt in on Malcolm's chapter, but as I've read this I thought it may help you to hear from me. Here is my point of view of exactly what I've put Malcolm through! There have been times when I have shouted at him, asked him to leave the room, walked out on him and pushed him away. He has been there when the ache has simply overwhelmed me. He has coped with times of inconsolable crying and he has watched me kick things when I've got so mad that I needed to lash out! Malcolm has never once put me down. He has always seemed to know exactly what I needed, be it hugs, silence or some hard words. He was prepared to do what was necessary even though on occasions it was costly!

There was one bad evening after the miscarriage when I was devastated. We were both suffering. I was shaking with the tears and Malcolm turned to me and shouted. I looked at him and said, 'No. I can't do this; I can't handle you shouting at me too. We need some space.' Malcolm turned and walked away. I sat on the kitchen step hugging the wall. I couldn't move because the hurt of losing my baby and the moment of anger with my husband were all too much. Most men would have walked out, punched a wall or left the house – not Malcolm. Awhile passed and I fell asleep on the floor. Malcolm came back scooped me up in his arms and helped me to bed. He kissed me and stroked my head. 'It's OK,' he said reassuringly. I was horrible to him and yet he only retaliated with love. I can honestly say that I would not be alive today if it wasn't for Malcolm. He was my strength when I had none. When I couldn't pray he'd pray for me and with me. When the tears flowed he cried with me. When I laughed he laughed with me. (It wasn't always bad!) When I was disappointed he encouraged me, and when I asked for a hug there was always one available. I used to jokingly say that Malcolm was to give me hugs on demand – and he did! For me, as a woman, being told that I would never have children naturally was devastating. Malcolm cared for and went through everything with me. I was not alone even though sometimes I felt it. I praise God for a husband who never failed me, never let me down and stood by me whatever I was going through! Guys – you are so important to your wife. Don't underestimate how much you are needed!

8
INFERTILITY: EXAMPLES FROM SCRIPTURE

Often I have looked at different people's stories in Scripture and am so glad that these people's stories are there for us to read and to learn from. It is such an encouragement to see that infertility is not a new phenomenon! It encourages me because these were people living in a different society and century and yet there was still the pain, hurt and feelings that we experience today. These were real people living in real situations with real feelings, expectations and disappointments!

This chapter is really my comments on the stories of some of these people. I would recommend that you read these individual stories for yourself. It may be that as you read God's Word, something will strike you that I have not picked up on. You may come across something that is more applicable to your own personal situation. Please note that I am not a great theologian. There may be other incidents from Scripture that I have missed, but these are the ones that have hit me over these years and that I noted in the front of my Bible. These are simply my thoughts!

Abraham and Sarah (Gen. 15-18, 21)

They must be the most well-known couple in regards to infertility! This is a fascinating story. Read it and see how dramatically Sarah takes things into her own hands. She was desperate enough to set her husband up with Hagar, and look how pear-shaped that situation went. In these chapters we can read about the covenant that God made, how he gives Abraham and Sarah their names, and then there are the three special visitors. It is then that we find out about the miracle of Isaac's conception and birth!

Let me try and share with you some of the things that I have found helpful. Abraham, in Genesis 15:2, shares his situation with God. Even though God knows it already, he points it out to the Lord. His disappointment oozes from this verse as he describes who will inherit his estate. Abraham is crushed and yet he is honest with God. This is not easy to do. I don't think I can honestly remember a single time when it was. It is hard enough during our normal times to be honest with God, but when it is something close to your heart it can be even harder.

There is one thing about Abraham that I found interesting and lovely at the same time. When he was being honest with God, God wasn't mad at him for how he felt. He didn't have a righteous 'go' at him. In fact He does the opposite and repeats His promise (Gen. 15:4,5).

Abraham recognizes that children are from the Lord. In Genesis 15:3 he says to the Lord, 'You have given me no children'. This is a good place for us to start. Children are a gift from God. They are not earned. It's God who chooses who He gives the gift to and the timing of that gift! So often I have shouldered the responsibility of us not having children, where in fact I should have the attitude of Abraham who knew that the responsibility was God's!

Genesis 15:6 gets me every time I read it. 'Abram believed the LORD, and he credited it to him as righteousness.' Against all the odds Abraham believed the Lord, he trusted

God despite what his circumstances looked like. What a man of faith! We even see him mentioned a few times in the New Testament as an example for the believers in Galatians 3:6-9, 14 and James 2:21-24. However, my favourite New Testament reference has to be in Hebrews 11:8-12. Verse 11 in this passage is the one that is heavily underlined in my Bible. It says, 'By faith Abraham, even though he was past age – and Sarah herself was barren – was enabled to become a father because he considered him faithful who had made the promise.'

This man trusted God and trusted the character of God! It's not the people, the situation or even the promise that hits me in this verse – but the faithful God! Let's look at Hebrews 11:17. This is a reference to when God tested Abraham. (You can read the full account of this in Genesis chapter 22.) I have a note written in my Bible beside Hebrews 11:17 that merely says, 'What faith to be willing to sacrifice what he longed and waited for.' I know there is much more to this story, but it inspires me that Abraham was so sure of God. He had the Lord first in his priorities. For me I know there have been times when I have put conception before Christ, especially when we were going through hospital treatments with assisted conception. Yes, this challenges me. Is the Lord my number one priority?

Now, back in Genesis chapter 16 we see in verse 2 that it was Sarah's idea to get things sorted out by bringing Hagar into the situation. I'm sure that Sarah's recommendation would have hardly helped Abraham's faith. In Genesis 16:3 we see that it had been ten years since Genesis 13:1. It had been a long time and Sarah's plan seemed a good idea. Ten years had passed. The test of time seemed to blur Abraham's faith in God's promise. This can happen to us too. We need to be so careful not to lose sight of God's will over time. We need to watch that we don't step out of His best for our lives. This is easier said than done! Malcolm and I firmly believe that God has promised us a child. It was easier to believe and to hold on to that promise after three or four years. It was much harder for us to hold on to that promise after six or seven years.

In Genesis chapter 18 we read about the time when Sarah laughed at a conversation she was eavesdropping on. When I read this I have real compassion for Sarah. She had lost hope. She had lost sight of the promise. And the whole idea of her conceiving was now a joke. I wonder if you have ever been in that place. I know that Malcolm and I have. We have lost all hope of ever being able to have a child. We have lost sight of God's plan and His best for us. It's a tough place to be. If you are in that place where hope seems lost I would really encourage you to read Lamentations 3:1-20. We see the author is in dire straits. He is not in a good place. Then we get to verses 21-24, 'Yet this I call to mind and therefore I have hope: Because of the LORD's great love we are not consumed, for his compassions never fail. They are new every morning; great is your faithfulness. I say to myself, "The LORD is my portion; therefore I will wait for him."' The thing that hits me about these verses is that it is a choice. We have to make this decision to call to mind, to remember. The author's situation had not changed at all, but instead of dwelling on hopelessness the writer of Lamentations began to dwell on the Lord's love, faithfulness and goodness. Be encouraged if you are out of hope. Call to mind these things and see your tank for hope topped up!

Lastly in Genesis chapter 21, we finally see God's promise fulfilled and Isaac arrives. Verse 2 says, 'Sarah became pregnant and bore a son to Abraham in his old age, at the very time God had promised him.' The real and repeated encouragement for me is that God's timing is perfect – it really is! Again – an easy thing to write! There have been times when well-meaning people have tried to encourage me that God's timing is perfect. When I've been in the midst of treatment, or on day one of a late period, or two weeks after a miscarriage – these were not the times I wanted to hear that God's timing is perfect. At times like that God's timing is a mystery and one that we do not understand. This is where faith and trust simply *have to* kick in.

I hope you understand what I am saying. I don't glibly say that God's timing is perfect, I have to choose to have faith that God's plans are perfect and I have to trust Him in those plans and their outworking. As I write this I do not know whether we will ever conceive again. I do not know whether we will ever have a child who survives to full term, or a child that I will look at face to face. But I do know that I can trust God and I can have faith in Him if I choose to do so even in the darkest hours.

'I can trust God and I can have faith in Him if I just choose', sounds great, but it is when the rubber hits the road, the chips are down and things are tough that this really takes maturity to say and to feel!

Isaac and Rebekah (Gen. 25:21-24)

The first thing to note is that Isaac is Abraham's son! Now Isaac and Rebekah are barren too. We know that Isaac prayed and that God answered. This sounds so easy doesn't it! But I imagine that there was much seeking of the Lord. In fact in these few verses it says that Isaac asked on behalf of his wife. There have been times when I have been unable to ask the Lord for a child. There have been times when I've simply had enough and Malcolm has asked the Lord on my behalf. I wonder if this was the same for this couple or whether it is referring to the culture of the day where women who were childless seemed to be regarded with shame!

Jacob and Rachel (Gen. 29:31-35; 30:1-24)

This is a story of two sisters, Rachel and Leah. Their father tricked Jacob into marrying both of them instead of just marrying the one girl that he loved. This account reeks of envy, jealousy, a longing for love and desperation for a child. To grasp all that goes on in this story you really need to read it in full. We are told in Genesis 29:31 that Leah was not loved but that God opened her womb and enabled her to conceive. Rachel, however, who was loved by her husband, was barren. So begins Jacob's

large and complicated family! Leah has four
boys: Reuben, Simeon, Levi and Judah. I find her
comments after each child quite interesting:

> *Reuben – 'It is because the LORD has seen my
> misery. Surely my husband will love me now.'*

> *Simeon – 'Because the LORD heard that I am not
> loved, he gave me this one too.'*

> *Levi – 'Now at last my husband will become
> attached to me, because I have borne him three
> sons.'*

> *Judah – 'This time I will praise the LORD.'*

The first three concentrate on her lack of being
loved by her husband. It isn't till the fourth
son that she praises the Lord and doesn't even
mention her husband's love!

Now here is where we catch a glimpse of
what Rachel has been going through. She has
seen her own sister give her own husband four
children. She is jealous and she is desperate.

In Genesis 30:1 she has a 'go' at Jacob. 'Give
me children, or I'll die!' Jacob becomes angry
with her and replies, 'Am I in the place of God,
who has kept you from having children?' He
recognizes that her fertility lies firmly in God's

hands! So begins this story of surrogacy using her maidservant. This seemed acceptable in those days and even in verse eight after the second son, Naphtali, is born to Bilhah, we see Rachel rejoicing because she has won over her sister.

The rejoicing must have been quite evident to Leah because we then see a retaliation of surrogacy as Leah gives her maidservant, Zilpah, to Jacob. So at this point in the story we see Jacob with eight sons: four by Leah, two by Zilpah (Leah's maidservant) and two by Bilhah (Rachel's maidservant). Some time has now passed and Rachel is still childless. I wonder if she really was rejoicing in her heart as she looked at these eight boys!

Then in the midst of this rather bizarre story, where Jacob is juggling sleeping with four women and it seems his wives are counting their worth in the number of children that they produce, there comes this deal that the sisters make over some plants! This account is in Genesis 30:14-16. Reuben, Leah's eldest son, finds some mandrake plants.

'What's the fuss about these plants?' I hear you say. I wondered that too, so I looked it up! Apparently in those times mandrakes were renowned as a kind of fertility drug and also increased sexual desire. Anyway, they make this deal where Rachel asks Leah for the fertility plants and in return gives Leah the opportunity to sleep with Jacob. The plan kind of backfired on Rachel though when Leah became pregnant again with yet another son, Issachar. It didn't end there – yet another son was born to Leah, her sixth son, Zebulun. Time goes on and we see that some time later after these two boys she has another child, this time a girl – Dinah. Rachel's desperation when she saw the mandrakes as her answer and took the situation into her own hands has failed. Even after Rachel has acquired this 'fertility' plant it is Leah who has conceived and given birth three times!

Rachel must have been devastated. Her sister has seven children plus two by a maidservant. At last, though, we see Rachel with a son, Joseph (see Gen. 30:22-24). Rachel says, 'God has taken away my disgrace.' It's interesting that earlier on she had been rejoicing over the birth of Dan and Naphtali, but now we see that the disgrace was still there. Her children, up till now, had been through surrogacy alone. Shame and disgrace would have been hers still. Then we see Rachel ask the Lord to give her another son. This is not answered directly. In fact, it is quite some time later that we see her prayer answered. In Genesis 35:16-18 Rachel does give birth to another son named Benjamin. However, she dies as a result of the childbirth.

This is a long and complicated story, but it shows where envy, jealousy and basing your worth on the wrong things can lead. I have to be honest with you and say that I have struggled with all three of these – with envy, jealousy and basing my worth on having children. There have been times when I have been jealous of other women. I've struggled when I've seen women who fall pregnant as a result of sin. I've found it difficult to see people who seem to get married and have a baby straight-away.

Thankfully I dealt with those jealous emotions fairly quickly. Well, it was weeks rather than months! This was because I recognized that the feelings I had could make me bitter as well as crush and knot me up inside. However, this is an area that I still struggle with and I do keep a close check on times when I am in danger of falling into the trap of jealousy and envy. I still do get caught out though. This is when I need to learn and practise taking every thought captive! 'We demolish arguments and every pretension that sets itself up against the knowledge of God, and we take captive every thought to make it obedient to Christ' (2 Cor. 10:5).

The thing about jealousy is that the only person that it's really going to affect is you. It will affect your relationship with God and your relationship with your spouse as well as cause a kind of spiritual gangrene that needs to be dealt with as soon as possible. Don't leave it, because it will just get worse!

You may have a better way than I do of dealing with jealousy, but this is the way I have dealt with jealousy in my life.

Firstly, I acknowledge that it is a problem, recognize it's there if you like. Sometimes it has taken someone very close to point it out to me, usually Malcolm! Secondly, I pray about it, I am honest with God. In fact I am more blunt with God on this one. I tell Him who I'm jealous of and why, usually in that order, because the why does tend to make me cry! Then when I am able to I bring that feeling to the Lord and if there needs to be forgiveness then I ask for it. However, sometimes I've known there to be a jealousy that isn't hateful or bitter, just an ache – these times I've not needed forgiveness but assurance and healing.

Manoah and his wife: Samson's parents (Judg. 13)

We do not even know the name of Samson's mother. In fact we don't know very much about this couple other than what is referred to in this chapter. We do know that this was a miraculous conception. Not only was she sterile, but also an angel of the Lord appeared to her with instructions for the pregnancy and the child's hairstyle once born!

Manoah, the father, is my kind of guy. He hears all that his wife says about the angel's visit and then goes to the Lord and asks for another visit because he feels inadequate for the job. This highlights that it is all right for us to ask God when we aren't sure about something!

Isn't it astounding how this couple experience God being on their case first-hand. I have to say I find this chapter a little incomplete because it kind of misses out the parents joy when he is born. Perhaps this sounds a little irreverent? But verse 24 is very matter of fact – 'The woman gave birth to a boy and named him Samson. He grew and the Lord blessed him.' However I guess we see the joy and expectation earlier in the chapter. But what really strikes me is how this promised child came at a bad time for the Israelites. We just have to look at verse 1 to see that they were doing evil in the eyes of the Lord. We then see that the Lord comes and is with Samson in amazing and powerful ways. I can't really devote the time to going through the whole story in this book, so if you're curious you're going to have to read it in the Bible for yourself!

The thing that I want to point out to you is that God used Samson despite all his mistakes. In verse 5 it says that Samson will *begin* the deliverance of Israel from the hands of the Philistines, and boy did the Israelites need it! Who would have thought that from a sterile, childless couple could come a man who was key in the deliverance of Israel and who centuries later we would all know about!

Boaz and Ruth (Ruth 4:13)
This verse really hit me at a time when I was struggling with the 'It's my fault' syndrome! As I read over it in my time with the Lord I reread it several times. It says clearly, 'the LORD enabled her to conceive'. It sounds funny but it wasn't down to Ruth or Boaz. It was the Lord that enabled this child to be created! We do not know if Ruth had trouble in the past with conceiving, it doesn't say in Scripture, but we

do know that she did not have children from her first marriage. I cannot imagine what it must have felt like for Ruth when she lost her first husband, but I am struck again and again by her faithfulness, loyalty and love to her mother-in-law. Ruth honoured God and we see that God honoured Ruth! Obed was a true gift. We see the other women, in verse 14, praise the Lord and honour his grandmother, Naomi. We see too from the family line, recorded in verses 18-22, that Obed was the grandfather of King David. As a result of that he is also recorded in the genealogy of Jesus in Matthew 1:5. Ruth too is mentioned in Matthew 1 – an honoured woman!

Ruth was not selfish. She was humble. She was more concerned with others than with herself and her own situation. She put others first before even marriage or having children. She is a stunning example for me!

Elkanah and Hannah – Samuel's parents (1 Sam. 1)

Well here we are again, different couple, same God. In verse 5 we see that it was the Lord that closed Hannah's womb. It wasn't her fault. It was God's authority! I love Elkanah. He cherished his wife and did not despise her or criticize her for not having children. In fact he loved her so much that he gave her a double portion. His questions oozed love and concern: 'Hannah, why are you weeping? Why don't you eat? Why are you downhearted?' You can just sense his love for her. This guy is a goodie!

I love Hannah too. This is a woman who tells God how she feels. She hurt, she ached, her husband's other wife Peninnah had children, and if that wasn't bad enough she provoked and irritated Hannah as well. Gosh I'm glad I don't have that to cope with!

Hannah was broken. She wept, she prayed and we are told that this was in bitterness of soul. I can sympathize with Hannah. I can grasp something of her crying out. Her sacrifice once Samuel was born was huge! Again similarly to Abraham she had her priorities right and made a huge sacrifice. She gave the child that she had longed for, waited for, yearned for, wept for, ached for. She dedicated him back to the Lord. In verses 27 and 28 Hannah says, 'I prayed for this child, and the LORD has granted me what I asked of him. So now I give him to the LORD. For his whole life he will be given over to the LORD.' What an example of an exceptional, heartfelt sacrifice!

The other lovely thing about this sacrifice

is Elkanah's support. Even in the sacrifice that Hannah made her husband supports her. In verse 23 he says, 'Do what seems best to you'. This surely was a couple whose priorities were set on God, but their love for one another shines through as well.

The one person in this story that I could just hug is Eli. I know many people who comment on those 'greats' from the Bible that they want to meet in Heaven. Well for me I'd love to meet Eli! OK, so he makes a bit of a wild assumption to start with. But after a brief conversation with Hannah he shows tenderness. He confirms to her that God has heard her cry. I wish that we had more people like Eli today to speak tenderness and encouragement to hurting people in the church!

Eli struggled though in leading the people and even struggled with his own household, see 1 Samuel 2:22-36. His own sons were disobedient before the Lord and ignored the correction of Eli, but the lasting impression of Eli for me is that he had a heart of compassion and a heart for God. Strangely, we learn much from Eli through his death in 1 Samuel 4. Eli hears the news that his two sons have died and then on hearing that the ark of God had been captured he fell backwards off his chair and died (see 1 Sam. 4:17, 18). Eli's priorities are noted – the ark of God, the presence of God, was more important to him than his own two sons.

The Shunammite Woman (2 Kings 4:8-37, esp. 14–17)

We don't know much about the Shunammite woman but let's start by summarizing what we do know. She was a 'well-to-do' woman, she was hospitable, she feared God, her husband was old and she had no children.

Because of this woman's age this situation reminds me of Abraham and Sarah. In addition to that she was also honest with Elisha when he prophesied about the birth of a son. She objects. She does not want her hopes to be raised (v. 16). However, God fulfils the prophecy and a year later she held her son just as Elisha said she would. But the story does not end there. We see that the child dies and we see this woman display incredible faith. She does not sit down and mourn but places the child on Elisha's bed and without telling her husband why she is going to see the prophet she leaves in search of him. We see God do a miracle through Elisha. This woman's honesty, faith and courage are an amazing example!

Zechariah and Elizabeth (Luke 1)

This is another well-known couple in Scripture. They were upright in the sight of the Lord and they were both mature. Another hopeless case – or is it? The angel comforts Zechariah with these words in verses 13-17, 'Do not be afraid, Zechariah; your prayer has been heard. Your wife Elizabeth will bear you a son, and you are to give him the name John. He will be a joy and delight to you, and many will rejoice because of his birth, for he will be great in the sight of the Lord. He is never to take wine or other fermented drink, and he will be filled with the Holy Spirit even from birth. Many of the people of Israel will he bring back to the Lord their God. And he will go on before the Lord, in the spirit and power of Elijah, to turn the hearts of the fathers to their children and the disobedient to the wisdom of the righteous – to make ready a people prepared for the Lord.'

I love the initial sentence that the angel comes out with. The second line says your prayer has been heard. How often I have cried out to God and wondered if God has heard my prayer. Perhaps Zechariah had wondered too!

The other thing that I love about this visit from the angel is the promise that not only would they have a son but also that he would be *full* of the Holy Spirit *from birth* and that God would use him amazingly to bring many to Himself. John was to be a vital part of God's plan and He used a mature and childless couple to kick this plan into action!

The angel who appears to Mary tells her about Elizabeth's conception. And in verse 37 it simply says, 'For nothing is impossible with God.'

This is a good place for us to conclude this chapter. I was told that I would not conceive without medical intervention. However, in December 2003 I conceived naturally. The impossible was achieved. If God has done it once and for countless others He can and will do it again. Take courage my friend, surely our God is the God of the impossible!

9
FAILURE, SHAME AND DESPERATION

We all have different struggles. For me the biggest was the feeling of failure and the shame that it brought with it. I remember being about 11 or 12 and someone at school asking me what I was afraid of. 'Failure' was my reply. From this early age I had put an expectation on myself to do well, to succeed.

This was an issue that was to dominate the years of infertility. At every period, every disappointment, every treatment that didn't work, every time someone else had good news, waves of failure hit me. I could not do or achieve what everyone else seemed to be able to! I felt an unbelievable failure, worthless and useless. My self-esteem nosedived at every disappointment. I'd start to accuse myself that I had done something so terrible that this was a punishment. I was in a serious downward spiral and it was affecting my walk with the Lord, our marriage, relationships with family, friends, and even my work life. I'd look at family members with their children and would feel crippled by the feeling of failure that I could not produce another member of this family. The pain and hurt this induced is hard to put into words, and I am sure that members of our families who read this would say that they never thought of me as a failure. But I was telling myself this is how people were feeling. It was crushing!

I felt a failure at work, but this changed as I got a new boss who encouraged me and gave me more responsibility. He changed the way that I viewed myself at work and became a very good friend and support on the rough days! I do praise God for a boss who didn't smother me, didn't overprotect me, but was honest with me. He displayed such support to Malcolm and I in some very dark situations, especially after the miscarriage.

The thing about this feeling of failure is that it affected my whole being. There wasn't one part of my life that was not affected by this. It was crushing me from the inside out and frustrating Malcolm who saw a completely different picture than I did.

It wasn't until I did a 'Christian Maturity' course that I realized my feelings were actually whispered lies from the enemy. The course was at our church and was based on the *Victory Over The Darkness* book by Neil Anderson. I will never forget the evening that we covered it. I simply could not 'get my head round it'. I talked with others on the course without referring to the issue at hand – what should I do when the accusations that the enemy used were true!

I went round and round in circles thinking about what I believed and what was really the truth! The other major revelation to me was that I had made a desire, a goal. I longed for a child of my own but rather than keeping it as something that I wanted, it became something that I had to achieve. Parenthood became a goal, and as you know goals are always achievable – desires and longings aren't.

Even recently I found a list of goals for 1997. Under family there were four things:

1. Love Malcolm as best I can.

2. Keep house better.

3. Make time for my husband.

4. Have a baby!

Something that really I had no control over had been made a goal. No wonder I was crushed every time it didn't happen! Achieving a goal that has been set always carries an element of satisfaction and success. Not achieving a goal when we try and try to do it carries a feeling of failure, frustration and disappointment.

It is very hard but we need to try and only have goals that are in our control, things that we can accomplish. Anything that we want or long for should be kept as a desire or a longing. This is very hard to do, especially when it comes to things like infertility treatment. We entered into treatment with a goal of conception. The more we read and spoke to the medical profession the more possible the achievement of our goal sounded. When it didn't happen the failure was intense, the disheartening overwhelming and the disappointment crushing. It is so hard to grasp and even harder to keep in check but it is so necessary that we ensure our goals are achievable and that our desires are kept as desires and not made into goals.

The feeling of failure really came to a head just after the miscarriage where there had been text messages going back and forth between us and our pastor. The verse Job 1:21b that says 'The LORD gave and the LORD has taken away;

may the name of the LORD be praised' had meant a lot to me and I shared it with several people. It was a text message that I will never forget. Our pastor pointed out that it was the Lord that had taken away, therefore no blame could be apportioned to me. I took this in, but could not really accept it. I blamed myself hook, line and sinker! It is a truth that I am still learning to grasp without blaming myself or calling myself a failure.

As a friend of mine has reminded me time and time again 'I can't do what only God can do and I can't be blamed for what only God can do.' The truth of this sentence is so simple and yet at the same time so difficult to grasp when naturally we blame ourselves for things that are out of our control especially for me regarding infertility and also miscarriage.

A few days after the miscarriage I went into work to see my boss. On the way I passed quite a few people. I realized when we got in the car to leave that I hadn't been able to look anyone in the face. I had stared at the floor as we had walked through. I felt such a failure and so ashamed. The one time that success had happened I had failed in maintaining the pregnancy.

This festered for a day or so. A text I sent

read, 'I can't see a way to sort out the failure/
shame issue because its true/fact I have failed
repeatedly and am so ashamed. So I'm stuck.'

A text came back.

'Is it a fact? Sorry if this seems hard but
I just don't see it in my Bible. I see God as
sovereign and whether He gives children is in
His hands. Satan knows where we are weak.
In your situation many would blame God and
Satan attacks them that way. Satan knows that
he can't get you on that one so he's accusing
you to blame yourself. But he's a liar.'

This was all true and helpful but I just could
not see how to stop thinking something that I
believed was correct. That same day Malcolm,
our pastor and I sat and talked through these
feelings of failure and shame. It was so helpful.
One thing that hit both Malcolm and I was
when the pastor shared about those that he
had broken the news of our miscarriage to
– no one said what a failure I was. No one said
that we must be really bad people. In fact one
reply that he received he shared with us. This
is not the exact wording but we hope you catch
the drift: 'I just don't understand God's ways.
Sometimes God entrusts people with really
difficult situations.'

This reply hit us. It was a bolt of lightning to

Malcolm and me. It was a completely different viewpoint for me. I had been thinking about how people would see us. Instead I should have been looking to the sovereign God and asking Him.

This goes the same for infertility. It does not need only to be applied to miscarriage. But if we look at the way I felt during the years of infertility with the whole situation out of my control, God was in control then, just as He is now! After we had spent some time talking through these issues the two guys prayed for me. For the first time in over a week there was peace in my heart. I walked from the room with a lighter feeling. I still hurt and to a certain extent I still felt a failure – the difference now was that I realized it was a lie from the enemy that I needed to be free from. I was determined to get free from these accusations. I no longer wanted to believe that I was a failure. I wanted to be free.

With me this feeling started well before infertility but over the years of infertility it gradually got worse and worse. What started as a small whisper from the enemy became a major problem for me – to the point where I believed that it was true, an unquestionable fact.

Be aware of things like this, they need to be dealt with before they become as huge as they did for me. It ate away inside, getting worse and worse. If you had an illness that was quite common and easily treated you would consult a doctor and begin treatment. However, what if you thought that you would just leave it, 'surely it will get better by itself'. This would not be sensible. What if you did consult the doctor and decided not to bother with the treatment. You'd be crazy when something easily treatable could become a lot more serious. Please don't make the same mistake I did. Get it sorted early on. Don't let it become such a huge problem that you begin not to be able to see the way out. God will see you through. He will make a way out. I still trust Him to take me to that place of complete freedom from my own unreasonable expectations of myself!

We often hear about the verse in 2 Corinthians 10:5 which refers to '[taking] captive every thought'. This is a really big issue for us and probably for other childless couples who long for a baby. It is too easy to think things about yourself, about others or even about God that just aren't true. Although thinking things that aren't true isn't necessarily wrong, the problem is when that small thought takes root and can fester away! I have tried to learn to deal with wrong thoughts as soon as they arrive. It's not easy at all. In fact it is really, really hard! Just be aware that thoughts can be dangerous. They can kick start negative feelings which in turn can knot us up, stress us out, even lead us into sin, or as it did with me, the lie becomes so plausible that we believe it as fact and truth. I wish that some thoughts came packaged with a label on that said 'Handle With Care', then I may be more cautious in dealing with them!

OK, we'll move onto desperation now. I remember a few years into infertility I was talking to someone who was also struggling to conceive. We began to talk about women that would go into a hospital and steal a baby. (This was prior to all the security systems they have now.) I remember her saying that she would never do it, but that she could understand what would drive a woman to do it – that desperation. I've known the crippling desperation of trying to obtain something that I could never get. I know what it is like to be so desperate I would do anything, whether it be buying the latest vitamin miracle cure, getting the best thermometer, purchasing ovulation tests, saving for expensive treatments – whatever. I would have done *anything* to have a baby. I would have literally given my right arm to have a child!

In this time of desperation we looked into adoption. We received the pack from the council and were invited to attend an 'open day' for prospective adopters. I don't want to linger on this too much, but I need to share with you where we came to over the issue of adoption.

Firstly, we decided that if we were to adopt then God would have to make it *extremely* clear. We wanted complete assurance that it was right. If it was not God's will for us to adopt it wouldn't just affect our lives but also that of the child concerned. Yes, this is how we prayed. We really didn't want to step out of or miss God's best for us at the same time!

Adoption was a temptation especially for me. I saw it as an 'easy option' compared to hospital treatments. This was dangerous ground because 'easy options' are not always easy and they are not always right! In fact I have complete respect for those who do adopt. It certainly isn't easy. Adoption may be right for you, God may confirm that to your heart, but if you are thinking it through make sure that you pray through it thoroughly. We know it isn't right for us at the moment, but it may be a path that God has for us later down the line!

Don't let desperation blind you into taking things into your own hands, being selfish or not taking time out to consult God!

I've been desperate for a child. I've experienced it and yet I simply can't put it into words. There just aren't any words that you can use in a situation that you can't do anything about. You are so desperate to change this situation that it pulls you apart inside. The best way to sum it up is to quote the meaning of desperate straight from the dictionary: 'extremely serious; hopeless, reckless and ready to do anything'.

In September 2003 I found a different desperation that I can explain. I met with God as never before. I tasted of His goodness and it left me hungering after Him. This discontentment was not because of childlessness. It was a discontentment with 'going through the motions' of being a Christian. The song 'This is the air I breathe', whose chorus reads 'I'm desperate for you', was often on my lips. I needed God. I longed to be in His presence. He was what I was ultimately desperate for – not a baby. Yes, I still longed for a child but that was not all consuming. The consuming factor became being with Him, in His Word, praising, talking to Him. God was whom I was desperate for!

10
JOYS AND SORROWS –
BEING SATISFIED WITH JESUS

At the time of writing the medical profession classes me as infertile. I am classed by society as childless. God classes me as His daughter, His son, heir, precious, treasured and dearly loved. Whether Malcolm and I conceive and have a child or we don't, God's view of me will not change. God will always dearly love me.

A conversation from years ago still 'haunts' me (for want of a better word). I remember chatting to a young woman, same sort of age as me, in the same sort of situation. I asked her a question, 'Would you rather have a baby or Jesus?' She paused for a moment and then replied, 'a baby'. It hit me like a bullet. I don't blame her for thinking that way. In fact, I too have felt that way at times. So as a result of that conversation which has stayed with me for years, this chapter simply has to be in this book! You may feel that you would rather have a baby than know Jesus. I don't want to have a 'go' at you or put you down, all I want to say is, 'I know, I understand. Take courage you will not feel this way every day!'

One of the biggest mistakes that I have made is counting my worth in how many children I have. I have thought that parents, grandparents, brothers, sisters and even friends would somehow treasure us more if we had kids. This is such a lie and a tactic that the enemy uses a lot! He whispers lies until they are whispered so much and so often that we believe them and end up crushed in spirit, down on ourselves and even depressed.

It has been a long journey for me to come to a place where I can honestly say that I only want to be satisfied with Jesus. Childlessness and infertility can be all consuming. I have seen it in myself. I have seen it in others. I am not saying that it is wrong to want kids or that it is wrong to weep. But what is wrong is when it takes over our lives and our relationship with God gets pushed out. In actual fact for us this is an ongoing battle. When the rollercoaster takes a dip we end up looking down, but as the rollercoaster starts to ascend from that dip the G-force pushes our heads back and once again we can look up and are satisfied with Jesus.

I love the story of Shadrach, Meshach and Abednego in Daniel 3. They are just about to get chucked into a very hot situation – a fiery furnace! What do they do? They put God's honour first. They say to the king in Daniel 3:16-18: 'O Nebuchadnezzar, we do not need to defend ourselves before you in this matter. If we are thrown into the blazing furnace, the God we serve is able to save us from it, and he will rescue us from your hand, O king. But even if he does not, we want you to know, O king, that we will not serve your gods or worship the image of gold you have set up.'

They have complete confidence in God whatever the outcome – they know in verse 17 that God is able to save them, and we see in verse 18 that 'even if he does not' save them they will serve no other. They have complete faith and trust in the Lord. So I hear you cry, what does this have to do with infertility? Well as I would put it, 'I know that my God is able to give me a child or even children, however *even if He does not* I will still love Him, still praise

Him, still make Him number one in my life. I will find satisfaction in knowing Him.' This has taken me years to be able to say honestly, and even sometimes when things are tough I may not be able to say it wholeheartedly.

Another passage that is a challenge is Habakkuk 3:17-18: 'Though the fig tree does not bud and there are no grapes on the vines, though the olive crop fails and the fields produce no food, though there are no sheep in the pen and no cattle in the stalls, yet I will rejoice in the LORD, I will be joyful in God my Saviour.'

Habakkuk's prayer can be related to many difficult situations, but I feel a certain affinity with these verses because there is a lacking. There are no buds, no grapes, a failed crop, no food, no sheep and no cattle. For me there is no pregnancy, no child – but yet my cry ends in the same way, with a determination that I will rejoice and I will be joyful in my Saviour.

So here is the 'Nick Cameron version' of Habakkuk's prayer: 'Though conception never seems to happen, though my dreams and plans have repeatedly ended in disappointment, though after years my husband and I are still childless, though the heartache still remains and the tears flow, though I wish things would change and they don't, though we never got to see our child, even though at times I hurt so deeply yet I will rejoice in the Lord, I will be joyful in God my Saviour.'

It amazes me that even in the midst of heartache and pain we can go to our Saviour just as we are. We do not have to wait till we feel a certain way. There have been times when I have hurt so much and yet have managed to cry out to God and He loves me despite how I feel at the precise moment in time!

The thing that I have found a love for during these years is the Psalms. In fact if you flick through my Bible there is hardly a page without underlining, asterisks or comment. There are verses that I have clung to when all else seems so bleak. There are verses that have encouraged, verses that are promises and then verses that have challenged. I want to share with you Psalm 27:8, 'My heart says of you, "Seek his face!" Your face, LORD, I will seek.'

The reason for choosing this verse over some of the more encouraging and inspiring verses is the last three words, 'I will seek.' Note that this is a choice and also said with determination. This is what we need to do as Christians who are unable to conceive. We need firstly to choose, to decide. Yes, this is what I will do. I will 'go' for Jesus. I will seek Him only.

We also need to be determined. A wishy-washy, airy-fairy decision will only last you to your next period, next disappointment or the next piece of good news for someone else! Your decision will need to be rooted firmly together – husband and wife, hand in hand – choosing the same goal which is Jesus! If one of you chooses to really go for God and the other is struggling with that decision and you move off – it will only cause you to go in different directions and so further away from one another. Deciding to go for God, to be out and out for Him, is *not* a legalistic decision. I believed for some time that it was. Then one day God came in power to me and made my heart love Him so much that He was all I wanted. He became my heart's desire. Oh yes, I still wanted children. Yes, I still longed for that child to hold in my hands and praise God for. But my greater desire was to know Jesus more. A son or daughter is for life. Jesus is for eternity!

This is one of the hardest chapters for me to write because I know there are times, even recently, when I have received a 'blow'. There have been days when something has happened and there has been much weeping and a deep indescribable pain inside. I have felt an emptiness or incompleteness that I cannot put into words. I do not want anyone to read this and think, 'Oh she's just some super-spiritual nutter.' I still struggle. I still cry. I still have to ask Malcolm for a hug. I still ask God, 'How long?' I still let my peace be lost and need prayer ministry. There was even a time recently when I lost my peace to such an extent that it took two evenings of serious weeping before the Lord, lots of hugs from Malcolm and a very long phone call to my pastor before I was again in a place of peace, of wanting Jesus first, of being able to go to God and ask Him to speak afresh to me. The situation had not changed – the person who had just told me that they were pregnant was still going to have the joy that had been denied to me – the only difference was in me.

After love from my husband, wise counsel from my husband and pastor, and some prayer, my focus was back on God and He had soothed my pain, putting His healing balm on my wound. We found that over the years of our infertility we have struggled repeatedly over the same issues time, after time, after time. This has been very frustrating. It doesn't seem to get easier. The heartache continues. It is so hard because as a Christian surely we should be 'reigning in life' and on fire for God all the time! It is not easy to be satisfied with Jesus all of the time, but this is my desire that simply I would find ultimate satisfaction in Jesus!

Being captivated by Jesus, being consumed with a passion for Him, being touched afresh by His Holy Spirit, being astounded by His love has made this time so much easier! There was a time when I was just going through the motions. I was trying desperately to achieve all I was supposed to on the outside and then desperately hurting on the inside. However, God touched me in a way that meant I had a new top desire – a desire for more of Him. You would have often heard me say, 'More Lord' to some of my friends! The other prayer that changed after God touched me was, 'Right, child now please Lord.' Instead of that prayer demand came the most awesome prayer that someone ever shared with me. It struck a cord and became my heart's prayer and that was: 'Whatever Lord!' You will see later on in this book that this prayer was prayed even in the car on the way to the hospital when I was miscarrying – an awesome, challenging, exciting and very scary prayer to pray!

You may have experienced disappointment

as I have done. You may have had years of one disappointment after another. Well, I'll let you into a secret that I have discovered. If you go for God with all your heart and seek Him first, open to *whatever* He says or has, you *will not* be disappointed with Him. Even though your circumstances may not change, God remains the same!

Christmas 2003 I was pregnant without knowing it and it was about this time that I said to Malcolm that I needed to be satisfied with Jesus without children so that if God blessed us with children then I would still be satisfied! Our satisfaction with Jesus should not be based on whether or not we have children – after all His love for us is not based on whether we have children or not is it!

11
THE CHAPTER I NEVER THOUGHT I'D WRITE

This is an odd name for a chapter of a book, but it fits exactly. My heart's desire was to have a child and the promise of God would surely mean that when conception was achieved everything would go perfectly… Well this is the story of how it didn't!

I learnt much through the years of monthly disappointments and the pain of never being able to see that which I wanted so much. The strange thing is that when I first became pregnant I told several people that I would go through the years of infertility again. This was because I could see that God had done so much in us during those years. We were stronger people, we had a stronger marriage, not to mention that we had grown so much in God and learnt so much during those years!

But as I start this chapter it is only five days since the miscarriage and in those five long days I have learnt so much more. The experience has been one that I will simply never forget. I spoke to my sister yesterday. She had a miscarriage several years ago. She has six beautiful children but the one that she lost will never be forgotten. As we talked she said to me that I should really write a book. After her miscarriage she reached for the shelves of a local Christian bookshop and found nothing that helped. I found snippets that helped but no one frank enough and honest enough to share their story and point me to the Lord. This book, I pray, will do that for others in the midst of their pain. I sat on the sofa during the early hours of this morning and read part of the 'Coping with Emotions' chapter of this book. The bulk of it was written about five or six years ago and as I read it I felt that God really used it to meet me in the present pain. So God used my sister yesterday to confirm to me once again that this book is needed!

This is what happened on the 6th January 2004. We had suspected for a few days that I was pregnant but I had refused several times to do a test. They had *always* been negative before so why should this be any different? Well, we got in from work and I was in quite a 'let's have a laugh' mood and said that I would do a test. To our amazement it turned out positive! I checked the box because this was one of those tests from the hospital treatment days and over a year out of date. I was unconvinced but optimistic so we went straight to the local supermarket and purchased another twin pack! As we gazed at each other across the supermarket our eyes met and you could almost feel the excitement and anticipation in the air. No one else seemed to feel it, but we did! We rushed up the stairs on our return and I did the test again. We now had two tests that said we were expecting. We checked the boxes again.

'Is it really correct? Are you sure that window should have a dot and that a line?' Malcolm said to me, 'Are you sure you did it right?'

My reply came, 'How many ways are there to pee on a stick?'

We sat on the bathroom floor looking at one another in disbelief. We both felt so numb. I remember saying to Malcolm, 'This is huge!'

Having been through years of never needing

to know, I had thrown out my old diary with my dates and cycle in it. We had to sit down and try to work out the dates from memory! I hardly slept that night. I couldn't get off to sleep and when I eventually did I woke at 3 am and never went back to sleep. I thought through everything. I was so grateful to God but so worried that something would happen to the baby. Malcolm and I still could not take it in! We had our night off the next day and went to Mothercare. It felt so naughty! I had started to keep a 'kind of diary' from this week – just a book with my thoughts in it.

7th January says, *We still are so amazed and our minds have been going like crazy. God has been so good, so faithful. He is faithful to keep His promises. It's only the second day we've known and this child has already been prayed for loads and we already love it, boy or girl.'*

I went to the doctors on the Friday. He was so excited for us! We nicknamed the baby 'Peanut' and loved it already.

The normal things followed from there. Morning sickness, or rather, all-day sickness, midwife appointment, things through the post regarding free prescriptions, signing up for freebies, even buying a couple of things for the baby in the January sales. We told some people fairly early on. We really needed the prayer support and I was throwing up so much they must have been wondering if something was seriously wrong with me. Looking back now I am so glad that we did tell close friends early on. It gave them a chance to celebrate with us and not just share in our sadness when the baby died. Those early weeks saw cards of congratulations and gifts from so many friends and family who were simply delighted and shared in our joy.

When we got the date for the scan – I was so thrilled. At last after seven and a half years I was to catch the first glimpse of my baby. I would walk from the hospital with a photo. I would see this tiny precious life that was part of Malcolm and me. I was so excited, but at the same time I was a little scared. Would everything be OK? What if they were to turn round and tell me that it was a phantom pregnancy that I had dreamt several times would happen? All my fears were put aside though as I realized that, yes, we were going to have a baby and if it was not totally perfect it didn't matter because God was in control and He could heal or He could give us the grace. Anyway, to me, the baby would be perfect whatever because it was ours! I was in love with my husband more than ever and the love that consumed us for our child I cannot describe. We had waited so long for this moment and the love for our unborn son or daughter was totally unconditional. We had not seen the baby. We had not felt the baby move. We knew nothing of the character, not even the name. Names we had chosen seven years earlier now seemed dated! Yet we loved this child with our whole beings.

25th February and all had been normal. I had suffered a little first thing in the morning with sickness, but as I had been told so many times this is a good thing because your hormones are doing all the right things!

I went to bed early. I was tired but this was not unusual. I had been getting up for weeks in the night to go to the toilet – 'pee time' as we affectionately called it. So at 1am when I got up to go to the toilet nothing was unusual except for a little spotting. I called Malcolm and we both decided that it was so minimal that we didn't need to worry and so I returned to bed. I tossed and turned for ages. I was in a lot of pain but simply put it down to trapped wind!

Just before 3am I went to the toilet and to my horror there was blood everywhere. Something different passed from me and I exclaimed, 'Oh my goodness what was that!' (We later discovered that it was the baby.) I screamed for Malcolm who woke straightaway and we tried to phone the emergency doctor – no reply. I was surprisingly calm, but Malcolm's face was white with anxiety. Anyway we decided not to mess about and go straight to A&E. It was freezing as I got in the car. Malcolm scraped the ice off of the windscreen and I shook inside as my mind raced ten to the dozen. Malcolm got in the car and I simply prayed aloud, 'Whatever Lord, you are sovereign.'

'Whatever Lord', had been for me like a Nick version of Mary's prayer, 'Let it be to me according to your Word.' Mary was simply relying on God and obedient to whatever He had planned. The ultimate prayer for a Christian to pray is, 'Whatever Lord.' This was my prayer in the midst of the unknown and Malcolm said a loud 'Amen' as we pulled out of our parking space.

The pain continued on the way to the hospital and we arrived there at around 3.15 am. A nurse saw us within minutes. My blood pressure was very high. The pain was increasing and we were both very scared. After a urine sample I was put straight on a trolley and Malcolm held my hand as the pain came and went. We were hardly there any time when they moved me to a secluded side room in the main A&E department. Little did we know that this would be our solitude for the next eight and a half hours. The pain came in waves and was really intense at times; these bouts of pain were a couple of minutes apart and lasted for a couple of minutes.

The nursing staff were great and by 3:45 we saw a lovely doctor. She questioned me and then listened for the baby's heartbeat. The more she tried to find it the more I knew that the baby was dead. Our eyes met and I shook my head at Malcolm. I knew. The doctor saw the shake of my head and reassured me that the heartbeat may just be hard to locate. The blood loss had been so massive and the pain had been so intense that I could not see how the baby could have possibly survived. The doctor asked if I would mind if she did an internal examination to try and work out exactly where we were at. She carefully ensured that all was ready prior to the examination.

The blood loss had been quite substantial already and so the procedure was uncomfortable. Malcolm and I looked at one another with tears in our eyes and hands held tight. Before I knew it there was a huge rushing sensation and the placenta and much blood had come out.

I asked the doctor if there was any sign of the baby and she said, 'No. Don't look. Just don't look. I am sorry it was all just there. You have definitely miscarried. I am so, so sorry.'

The mass clear-up operation began and a drip was put up. There were even tears from the doctor and nurse. Malcolm and I were left to grieve alone. I cannot even write down how I felt. Emptiness consumed but came with a deep love for my husband. By this time both hands had plasters where they couldn't get the line in. I was cold outside and in – a void unspeakable. The child that had been inside me for the last fourteen weeks was gone. We had been reading the pregnancy books on how the baby was growing. We knew that two weeks prior to this our baby would have been fully formed. The emptiness I felt is indescribable.

Some time later a senior house officer (SHO) came and asked us yet more questions. She seemed to lack confidence, which rubbed off on us! She also wanted to do an internal and was little prepared for the quantity of blood that I was losing. She stood there after the exam dripping with blood and requiring Malcolm's assistance to get her out of her very sticky situation. There was blood everywhere – walls, bins, floor, trolley and sink, all over me – everywhere. After she had left, Malcolm sorted me out and he pinched some clean sheets while no one was looking!

The pain had gone by now, but for a broken heart and a crushed spirit – disappointment had once again reared its ugly head. It never gets easier!

At 5ish my concern was more for others – family and colleagues – I ached for those who had shared our joy and been delighted to see an answer to their prayers.

Malcolm and I wept together on and off. The bleeding continued. The drip made my left arm icy cold. Our next 'visitor' was the doctor who took details of my scan that was booked for 11am and he explained that I would still have this scan to ascertain whether or not I would need any surgery. We were told several times that we would be moved to a ward but this never happened. There wasn't a bed anywhere for me so we remained in our little bay, which was fine for us.

Around 9.15 Malcolm had to go and move the car. He also needed food and I needed some tissues! So he left me with the breakfast that they had brought me. Whilst he was gone and I was alone, all I could do was cry. Loneliness and heartache overwhelmed me, but at the same time the song that went through my head was 'You give and take away – my heart will choose to say, Lord, blessed be your name'. This was our song. No matter what, we trusted in a sovereign God. Malcolm arrived back. I was delighted to see him and so full of love for my man. We talked more and wept again.

Malcolm's mum arrived and sat with us until they took me to antenatal for my scan. We made the long journey with me in a wheelchair, wrapped in blankets, pale, hair bedraggled, drip in tow and an A&E nurse accompanying us. I was glad that we took the staff route as it meant bypassing the 'waiting room of despair'. The nurse checked me in and the scanner staff reassured me that they would be as quick as possible. The moment that only a week before we had been so thrilled about was not as I had dreamt. I was almost longing for a living baby to appear on the screen, instead a sight that was not uncommon to us in the past – *nothing*, a void, blankness and *nothing*. There was only swelling and masses of blood, but the one and only consolation was at this stage no surgery would be required.

After a much-needed trip to the toilet and some attention from the nurse as my drip tube had become full of blood we waited for the porter. We waited for quite a while and I watched all these pregnant women and excited couples arrive for their scans. It brought memories flooding back – everyone else but never me – I was desperate to get out of there and back to the safety of A&E. The nurse who was with me could see how hard it was for us to watch all the expectant parents and decided that she would push me back to A&E. En route we met the porter who took over. I was so relieved to leave that area of the hospital that was full of so many painful memories.

When we eventually arrived back at A&E they had moved me to a room with a bed. It was warm and luxurious compared to the trolley and cubicle that we had been in. I was exhausted physically and emotionally. The bed was so comfortable and I longed for the unconscious state of sleep where I could forget the last hours, but although my eyes shut sleep never came. The doctor came to see me and informed me that I could go home on the condition that I returned in a few weeks for a scan to ensure that surgery was not required. They removed my drip, and my clothes and I were reunited. Malcolm's dad, who had arrived while we were at antenatal, drove Malcolm to get his car. I was free – I could go home!

I cannot remember the journey home. It felt like everything was a dream and I was just a spectator of the events around me. However, when we walked through the front door reality hit me like a concrete block on a raw egg! We had anticipated a day in August returning from the hospital with three in the car and this was no longer going to happen. The full force hit! I spoke to my parents to let them know that we were home and that we had definitely lost our baby. They said they were on their way to the station to get a train to come and see us. We were both so tired but Malcolm tidied up before the arrival of my parents and I went to bed. I was so tired, but I could not sleep. The more I cried – the more my head hurt. The more my head hurt – the more thoughts ran through it. The more thoughts – the more I cried. It was a never-ending circle of overwhelming heartache. After awhile of listening to my sobs Malcolm came to the bedroom and lay down next to me. Holding my hand and stroking my forehead he prayed and committed our treasured baby to the Lord. We held each other close and both wept. In time we both drifted in and out of consciousness until something woke us. A short while later my parents arrived – they stayed for a few hours – Malcolm looked exhausted!

After they left we simply just wanted to 'be'. The phone had been ringing all afternoon. Tears came at odd moments, with nothing in particular setting them off. I had no idea what to do with myself and paced back and forth from the dining room to the living room. I wish I had been able to say 'Goodbye' and we talked this through along with a 'keep-sake', which we decided should be a ring. The sooner we could get this the better.

Malcolm needed to go to work for a short while that evening but as he left to go I was overwhelmed. I didn't want to be alone. I wept and wept. When his parents called to say that they were nearly at our house he left. After awhile the doorbell rang and I assumed that it would be them. Instead there were some friends at the door. They were to be 'adopted grandparents' to our baby. They had brought plants and a card from work. I was so glad to see these two special people. Joy and I are close friends and she has been through so much with me over the last seven years. Malcolm's parents arrived while they were still here. I read the cards that had been brought and wept. I was so touched by people's love and kind words! Malcolm returned bearing his own gifts from a nearby pizza take-away – what a tremendous blessing!

The evening was a hotchpotch of phone calls, tears, hugs and food! I wrote the events of the day down at 3.30am. I had been up for over an hour. I was unable to sleep and was also aware I was keeping Malcolm awake. He was shattered and I needed to let him sleep – he had to be strong enough for both of us. I was worried for him. Part of my 'diary' says:

I know that we have a lot to work out, but he has much to carry as the bloke and yet he still needs to grieve. We are a unit – you can't have one without the other. We have to work through all of this together with God's help. You know today (well yesterday now) someone said that if they were in my shoes that they would be so angry with God but I'm not angry – I love my Heavenly Father and I trust Him unquestioningly. It doesn't mean that I don't ache and that I'm not upset – of course I am. It simply means that He is sovereign. He has proved to us that He can do miracles and I am convinced that He will keep His promise and show us that He can maintain a miracle! When I found out I was pregnant I told someone that I hadn't realized that you have to trust God for an answer to prayer, but you then have to trust God with the answer to that prayer. I trusted Him – some may read this and say that I made a mistake – NO definitely not – I trusted in the sovereign God 24 hours ago, 48 hours ago and I still trust

Him. He will be my comfort, my strength and my song. When all hope is lost I'll call Him Saviour. He will do what He will do and I will love Him whatever. So let it be to me according to your word – whatever Lord!

So that was the events of the day that we will never forget. I needed to put this in so that we can put into context how we dealt with the aftermath of such an experience. If you have had a miscarriage, I pray that this chapter will give you someone to identify with. You are not alone. We only discovered after the event how many people have been through this but no one (understandably) talks very openly about it.

12
EARLY DAYS AFTER THE MISCARRIAGE

The thing that strikes me about miscarriage as I sit here and wonder quite where to start is that the intense physical pain of the miscarriage for me only lasted about four hours. The physical uncomfortableness and readjustment for my body lasted a few weeks, but the emotional pain went on for much longer. As I write this it is only seven weeks since we lost our baby and the last seven weeks have contained many different emotions, feelings and masses of tears. I cannot say how long the hurt, pain, grief and rawness will last, but I can say that no matter how I feel, God does not change. I may be up and down like a yo-yo but He will be my constant and has been! I've searched desperately for answers these last weeks and longed for the ache to disappear. I have felt total despair, seen spiritual numbness and asked God many questions.

The one thing that I have discovered repeatedly in this time is that people share their own experiences of miscarriage or loss of a child either in cards, phone calls or in person. They can sympathize to some extent and this can be helpful or unhelpful! I found it very hard when someone shared with me what had happened to them when their baby died during the birth. I ended up hurting for them along with trying to deal with my own hurt and pain.

Malcolm and I talked long and hard about this book because we didn't want it to appear that we were telling others how to handle infertility and miscarriage. This book is merely our story, our experiences, and hopefully some of it will help you if you are going through a similar situation. It may also give you insight if you have a friend or family member facing the same issues. This chapter in particular is *not* how you should feel after miscarriage or how you should cope or what you should do. It is simply what happened with us and how we faced things. Each of us is different and everyone's circumstances are different. There is no wrong or right way to handle this tragedy. We found you have to go with the flow!

We felt that we handled things wrong or abnormally at times, but there have been numerous times when people have said to us, 'this is normal, this is OK'. Malcolm will also tell you that a handful of good, close friends have also said, 'Don't be so hard on yourself.' I would kind of beat myself over the head with things like: 'You aren't coping well. You should be doing better. Why can't you just pull yourself together.' This didn't help at all and ended up getting me screwed up in knots inside. 'Don't be so hard on yourself!' It's easy for me to say but it's hard to do. Try not to judge yourself on your 'coping ability' as you come to terms with the loss of a baby!

Malcolm and I were quite fortunate in the timing of the miscarriage. In many ways God had His hand upon us even in this terrible situation. The timing meant we had a few hours to talk, cry and just 'be' together before any other family or friend knew. The hospital staff were brilliant and left us alone as much as possible. We had this time together and we decided together that we would never forget our oldest child lovingly nicknamed 'Peanut'.

For me I needed something to help me, something precious to keep forever. This may sound a bit sentimental but I knew that for me this would help me to get through. Later that day Malcolm suggested a ring and I agreed!

The day after we lost the baby we went to a local jeweller and Malcolm saw a ring in the window that was just right. There were two colours of gold linked by a single small diamond. It fitted perfectly and was just beautiful. This ring is so special to us both and we will treasure it. That afternoon our pastor came to see us – we just chatted, wept and he prayed for us. It really helped for us to talk to someone outside of the immediate family – someone we both trusted, who knew us and was not judging us. Both Malcolm and I wept as we talked. He encouraged us not to bottle things up but to be open and real with one another.

The grief was consuming at times and meant that I had problems sleeping. At one point in the middle of the night I sat down in our rocking chair and tried to pray. I couldn't speak for the lump in my throat. I sat there aching from the inside out, staring at nothing and feeling the tears steadily flowing down my face. Eventually I decided to write down my prayer – what I would say if I could speak to God face to face. I didn't know what else to do with myself in the pain of it all. I'm so glad that I wrote this down as I've prayed it time and time again over the last seven weeks. This prayer has allowed the grief and hurt to flow as I have cried out to God and refocused on Him. I have let Him minister to my heart.

A verse that hit me in the first days and has been a constant blessing to Malcolm and me is Job 1:21b, 'The LORD gave and the LORD has taken away; may the name of the LORD be praised.' Our pastor pointed out to me that it wasn't just the fact that the Lord gave but it was also THE LORD that took away. Therefore no blame, fault or shame should be put on myself because it was the Lord. This has helped time and time again over these past weeks.

The early days saw me unable to make decisions. I couldn't decide what to wear, what to eat, where we should go, what I should do. Malcolm had to tell me things like this! I was often scared of being alone or being at home. The park became a place of refuge. On the Saturday after we had lost the baby, very early in the morning, I sat on a swing looking across the park. The air was fresh, the morning silent, my being was empty as I gazed across the field and let the tears roll down my cheeks. I sat alone, weeping. My heart was broken and consumed by an indescribable void and pain. Believe it or not it really helped me to be outside, alone and free to cry. I returned home feeling better for the 'space' to grieve!

Now, let me share some more of my diary with you. This is quite literally what I wrote at the time, so please excuse some of the details. I almost want to apologize for some of the things that are said here and have been tempted to 'crop' my entries, but if this is to help others then I need to be open and real. So this is simply what happened and this is how we felt…

Sunday 29th February 2004

Pete came this afternoon. It was the most helpful conversation we had found since the baby's death. I think because we were both aware that we needed to talk we were able to do so quite naturally, nothing was forced. Several large issues were covered as we talked. For me the biggest being that I had not seen my baby – the regret I felt on not taking the time to discover what I had lost here at home. I felt so cross with myself. I had denied both of us the chance to see our baby and I had denied our baby a proper 'goodbye' and place of rest. I can't explain fully the extent of my feelings on this and to be honest I am not going to try because as I opened up with Malcolm and Pete on this issue God brought a sense of closure over this regret. It was like a heaviness was lifted. Both guys did not blame me for not realizing it and neither condemned me for how I was feeling. Pete felt that I needed to take my focus from the baby's grave being a sewer to the fact that our baby is now with the Lord. He felt that one way to help in this is for Malcolm and I to say 'Goodbye' properly and that somewhere with water would be a good idea. So at some point this week, one evening, we will go to Tower Bridge with a couple of white tulips – one from Daddy and one from Mummy and we will pray and say our goodbye properly. After Pete had gone both Malcolm and I felt a difference – not such an oppressive heaviness. This confirmed to Malcolm's heart, especially, that when Pete returns from the Life In The Spirit Conference we should talk to him together again.

The really tough thing today has been physical. I sat in the garden bundled up in hat, coat and gloves and read for a little while but on coming in I was in pain – then Pete arrived and while he was here I went to the toilet and could not move. The blood flowed as urine would. I couldn't believe it and it shook me. The other physical thing today is that my breasts have been 'leaking' – I have found this so upsetting. No one had warned me about this and it has been quite emotional realizing that my body thinks it has given birth!

Alasdair and Hilary popped in this afternoon and shared with us what was said to the family at Lansdowne. Just as in Joseph's story when you come in at different points it is full of hopelessness and is very dark e.g. when he was in prison,* so for us this is just mid story and simply a dark chapter.

Nicole rang tonight and we chatted for a while. She caught me at a good hour and God's grace was visible to her over the phone. While I was talking to her Martyn arrived with a bouquet of iris' and lilies from all the Spurgeon's students and a beautiful card. He also brought some Pot Noodles and chocolate from him and Sarah. They must know us well – people are so kind!

Forgot to say about the letter to our families that we have written. We got PD to read it while he was here and he said that it was good, honest and brave.

Monday 1st March 2004

So today is Monday – Joy from work is coming to have lunch with me and we go to Hilary's for dinner. It is 4.12 am now and I've been awake for some time. It seems to be that I wake around the

---

* Genesis 39–40

time we miscarried – weird huh?

Me again – just found my 'book' and read a chunk. I was struck again by something I wrote years ago – Job 1:22 'In all this, Job did not sin by charging God with wrongdoing.' He lost everything! Me I have only lost one child. How dare I even consider that God has messed up? How dare I even contemplate being angry with God? Also Job 1:21b 'The Lord gave and the Lord has taken away; may the name of the Lord be praised.' I texted this verse to Pete. He texted me back to point out that I haven't failed. It is the Lord who has taken away.

It has been an odd day. This morning I did not bleed at all and this afternoon I passed several large masses. It felt like I was miscarrying all over again. The bleeding was heavy all evening and to get me out Malcolm took me for dinner to his Mum's. His brother David was there too and I was so glad to see him. When he left I asked him for a hug. It was a struggle to hold back the tears. I was so grateful for this hug from my brother-in-law!

Tuesday 2nd March 2004

The night was horrible. We were both awake at 1.30 am and Malcolm asked me if I needed to talk. So we sat in bed and chatted for a while. Malcolm prayed and then sleep eventually returned.

I woke feeling like the raw egg being hit by the concrete block all over again. I hurt so much. Pastor Pete phoned and we talked. I explained that I had allowed myself to soar and crashed to the earth with an enormous thud. My whole being was smashed and I could not fly – in fact I didn't want to – I was scared to fly again!

Pete gave me an example of a child who falls from a bike and to start with the father holds the back of the bike – confidence needs restoring – and eventually the father lets go so that the child can ride once again. After the call I lay in bed looking at the ceiling and then it hit me. There was no quick fix but Father God, who is so loving will take me one bit at a time.

Malcolm and I were trying to handle the next weeks, next months and in fact the next six months left till the due date. God wants to lead us to handle one moment, one hour, and one day at a time until our confidence is restored and healing can begin.

Wednesday 3rd March

Woke up this morning and decided to go and see my boss with my doctor's certificate and explain where we are at re sick leave, scans, possible surgery etc. Malcolm was taking the day off, as he needed some space. This meant that he could come with me as my husband rather than a work colleague! It was around 9 am when I was showered, breakfasted, dressed etc. I was getting more and more anxious about it so Malcolm decided that we should just go. Stepping over the threshold was huge!

I walked into the office and Paul, my boss, was there.

'I've come to see you, we need to have a chat,' I said.

He gave me a massive hug and we went to his office. He was so good and so supportive and loving. After the meeting was over we saw Joy and Amanda. There were only about a dozen students around but it overwhelmed me – all these people! I could not lift my head from looking at the floor. I felt so full of shame and I daren't catch anyone's eye! As we left we saw Geoff, the maintenance guy. I could see he didn't know what to say or do so I walked over and just said, 'Well do I get a hug then?' He gave me a massive hug! Malcolm asked what I wanted to do and I knew that I could not just return home so we went for a walk around South Norwood Lake. Later on we went out to lunch with Malcolm's Mum and just pottered really. This afternoon saw more flowers arrive. They are really helping both of us – the dining room table is covered now and the smell is fantastic.

It has been very hard today as we kept thinking this time last week we were so excited about the scan, the Summer, the rest of our lives etc etc! The early part of this evening saw us go up to

Tower Bridge. We each wrote cards to attach to two single white tulips. We did this separately and then shared what we had written. It was so hard and gutting to sign 'Mummy' and Malcolm said the same about signing 'Daddy'. We walked to the middle of Tower Bridge, we both prayed and cried then we threw our tulip into the water. 'Bye Peanut, Goodbye my baby,' I whispered under my breath. We stood there in the cold; the sound of the traffic seemed to disappear in the silence and numbness of our grief. As we walked back to the car I was relieved that it was over but the finality of it and the emptiness hit me. I said to Malcolm, 'I don't know how to explain this and I don't want to upset you, but there is a part of me that just does not want to keep on living – I don't want you to say anything, I just want you to know.' On the way back we went to Burger King. We were both cold, hungry and I was desperate for the toilet!

Tonight was the first evening that I really couldn't cope. The tears rolled down my face as I repeated to Malcolm, 'This is too hard, I can't do this.' I wanted to leave the planet. I couldn't see any way ahead. Malcolm felt numb and empty and I asked him not to touch me. I didn't want hugging or kissing – just to be alone. He left me to grieve on my own. Not more than five minutes later I realized how awful I had been to my man and went downstairs and apologized. We hugged.

Thursday 4th March

It is now 4.39am and I have been up for ages. I keep thinking 'this time last week'. I looked in the mirror as I came downstairs – my eyes are red and puffy from the tears shed last night.

Re being pregnant again: Part of me never wants to be again. I'm scared of letting my hopes rise, of disappointment yet again, of loving a baby so much only for it to be stolen by miscarriage again. The other part of me wants to be pregnant a.s.a.p. – arrggh – I just don't know!

Went to Jim and Nicole's this evening for a meal (we had set this date weeks ago) I felt physically sick on the way and had a massive panic attack but once we were there I was fine!

I am so, so tired though – the lack of sleep is crippling!

Friday 5th March

Today I just keep crying. I feel such a failure and so ashamed. How can I ever get back to 'normal'? I ache in my very depths, I feel so messed up. I know that I should be strong; trust in the Lord and have grace, but I can't work it all out with the way I feel. My insides feel smashed and empty. My excitement for the future is, as Anne of Green Gables would put it 'a graveyard of buried hopes'. Dare I ever hope again? Dare I ever dream of holding a child that I may call son or daughter? I simply want to step off of the planet and return when laughter is in the air. This whole experience has so knocked me – confidence gone, hopes shattered – I feel broken for family and friends too.

I'm desperate for someone to pray for peace in my heart. I'm desperate for the Lord to calm the waters in my spirit. The voices in my head all point the finger and push me downwards, I feel so depressed. I don't think my faith is strong enough, but I know God is strong enough. He is going to have to touch me Big Time! The pain deep inside is so intense today. The realization that I will not be holding a son or daughter this year has hit me. My hopes are not just deferred they are destroyed. There isn't one part of me that can see a way through. My options are limited – keep going or wither! Today I feel like just withering – I need a giant miracle.

Monday 8th March or Tuesday 9th March?

Spent the morning typing up chapters from the book. I was so challenged and encouraged. I texted this to Malcolm and Pete:

'Just read something that I wrote last year. If you have kids tomorrow God's love for you will be just the same as it is now with no kids. Can't text it all but it goes on to say no matter what, God will still be there – no matter how great or bad things get – He is constant. Let your delight

be in eternal things rather than passing things. Wow I wrote this too: Medics class me as infertile, society classes me as childless, God classes me as daughter, heir, precious, treasured, dearly loved. Wow!'

Wednesday 10th March

Go today to my Mum and Dad's. Went to the Bible Study last night. I was shaking! Malcolm and I spoke for a while last night. I am struggling with two things:

1. How quickly things have changed – from being content and satisfied with God – to this. Also the dreams and excitement of this year, all the longings finally being seen and realistic have changed to dreams crushed and a discontentment, a desire to have a child NOW just like when we were going through treatment. I feel like I have gone backwards.

2. The fear of hope. Sounds weird but I am afraid to hope that I will ever become pregnant again. I'm afraid of loving another baby like Peanut only for the same thing to happen again, but I'm scared at the same time of not letting myself love another baby, depriving that baby of love. My brain is so confused! I am worried too for Malcolm because I can't explain how I feel to him and I think that it's hard on him. I feel like someone has ripped out my heart – my very core, stomped all over it and put it back.

Met our newest niece today for the first time. Hannah is a few weeks old now and she is beautiful. I held it together quite well. Sounds strange but the hardest thing was seeing Malcolm hold her. He would make such a good Dad and I ache that he has lost this baby. I love my husband so much. I long to be able to hand him his own son or daughter rather than a niece or nephew!

I am terrified re the scan (this was to ascertain if there were any 'retained products' and decide if I was going to need surgery). Part of me wants them to say that it was all a mistake and that we are still going to have a baby (totally unrealistic) and the other part of me is scared stiff of the prospect of surgery, cysts or complications. I long for this scan to be a full stop rather than a comma, semi-colon or exclamation mark!

On top of this is the wish that I had dreamt all this and that it never really happened. I wish I could turn the clock back to December. I almost wish that the pregnancy hadn't even happened. Then I feel bad about that because Peanut was a person, a human, a life. How dare I wish another had never existed – Aargh I just can't take this!

Sunday 14th March

After being at Mum and Dad's it was very hard to return home last night – so many memories – the bathroom and bed in particular. There were many tears Saturday night and I didn't sleep well.

Today we went to see Peter and Emma. I had some time with Emma alone. It was so helpful to ask her lots of questions from her own experiences of miscarriage and just to talk. God did quite a lot of repeating. Things that had already been said were said again: God sometimes entrusts us with difficult situations; unhelpful thought patterns from the past; God giving me a new heart along with the promise that it's a new day. He is going to do something new!

Monday 15th March

Didn't sleep well at all last night. I'm so worried about the scan!

This morning saw God do a miracle with traffic and parking to get to the hospital. I was first on the list. Malcolm had to work so Margaret came with me. I was so glad she was there! All clear: the full stop that I had been praying for – not a comma or exclamation mark! Praise the Lord!

I was shattered this afternoon. I think the lack of sleep combined with the emotions of the hospital appointment took it out of me!

Tuesday 16th March

Didn't sleep well at all last night. I'm so worried about going back to work!

Tuesday morning and what a panic re going back to work. My reading was in Psalm 118. WOW What a Psalm!

Verse 5: 'In my anguish I cried to the Lord and he answered me by setting me free.' – A promise for me.

Verses 6-9: 'The Lord is with me; I will not be afraid. What can man do to me? The Lord is with me; he is my helper. I will look in triumph on my enemies. It is better to take refuge in the Lord than to trust in man. It is better to take refuge in the Lord than to trust in princes.'

Verses 13-14 'I was pushed back and about to fall but the Lord helped me. The Lord is my strength and my song; he has become my salvation.' These were so encouraging!

Verse 24 made me laugh: 'This is the day that the Lord has made; let us rejoice and be glad in it.'

Verses 28-29: 'You are my God, and I will give you thanks; you are my God, and I will exalt you. Give thanks to the Lord, for he is good; his love endures forever.' These last verses reminded me of Job 1:21b.

Work was OK I felt weird, like I was dreaming, everyone seemed distant! I did OK until the postman came and gave me a hug! Half days until next week so this afternoon I went at 2pm to see Pete at the Church. A light bulb has finally come on in my life. I realize that the way I view how others think of me and how I think of myself is wrong.

I have the feeling of being in a hurdles race and in my lane the next hurdle is actually a brick wall – no way round, no way over, no way through! I can't go beyond this point. I'm stuck. So I'm sitting on the track watching others move on, trying to work out how to get through this. Pete and I talked through this.

He has given me three things to do:

1. I am to get it in my head who I am in Christ, keep reading it aloud.

2. Ask God to show me what these bricks are and to also show me what the cement holding them together is.

3. Ask God to give me a glimpse of beyond the wall to give me the desire to go ahead and tackle it rather than leave it.

As Pete prayed after we had finished talking a lot, what he prayed was spot on. The picture came to mind that what I am going through is like a visit to the opticians. You know how when you have your eyes tested they slide lens discs in and out. Some of them obscure your vision. A lot of things can get slotted in obscuring my 'spiritual vision'. I have to deal with words and feelings like guilt, worthless, useless. These words need removing so that eventually the glasses can go too! When we were thinking about this picture we thought about the chart that you see on the optician's wall and how that chart will have words on the very bottom line that you are to try and read. We thought about how the words that God has revealed on the very bottom line of his wall chart are 'I love you because...' He doesn't include a reason after those words. He loves me not because of who I am or what I've done – just because!!

It is now Tuesday night and I have just read Titus 3:4–7. These verses have such a WOW factor! 'But when the kindness and love of God our Saviour appeared, he saved us, not because of righteous things we had done, but because of His mercy. He saved us through the washing of re-birth and renewal by the Holy Spirit, whom He poured out on us generously through Jesus Christ our Saviour, so that, having been justified by his grace, we might become heirs having the hope of eternal life.'

Wow – I have written in my Bible – 'Our God is a Generous God.'

Thursday 18th March

Today has been a terrible day. I don't really know why but I struggled at work and was 'down' all evening. Eventually a cord snapped and the tears flowed. I couldn't stop crying. Despair set in and the ache consumed – terrible night! This is so horrible!

Sunday 21st March

Mother's Day – need I say more?!?

Saturday 3rd April

My period came today it caught us unawares as from what the medical profession told us we thought it would be another week or so. I can only describe these past few days as really dark days.

Sunday 4th April

Church brought many tears and I sat after the service in Nicole's arms sobbing. I'm broken, so crushed, destroyed! I described it to Nic as though I were a Ming vase that had been dropped and was in so many pieces that it would be impossible to get back together! I've had enough of hurting. I don't want to hurt anymore!

Monday 5th April

This is the first time in all of this that I've questioned God, questioned His character even. Neither of us is in a good place spiritually. This is a very low and dark time. We really need intervention. Malcolm and I talked for some time this evening and I admitted to him that I couldn't even talk to God right now. I'm so, so broken. It's almost as if I lack spiritual energy. I am too weak from this tough journey.

Tuesday 6th April

The ache inside is huge. It throbs away unceasingly. We are both OK at work. We just keep busy but at other times things are not good at all. Yesterday when we left work we were snappy with one another. The strain of our pain is showing at times. We need help to get through these dark days. Malcolm is going to send an e-mail to trusted friends asking them to pray and stand with us in this darkness.

Thursday 8th April

I'm still really low and I'm not talking to God at all. Malcolm has had a real breakthrough. He seems to have broken through the darkness. He knows that I can't pray at the moment and is praying for me!

Saturday 10th April

We were at the Church for the outreach today. Malcolm was getting stuck in but I was still really low and to be honest am not sure why I bothered to go. It has been a terrible week. After my period had come I was depressed, distraught, gutted. It has been a very, very, dark week.

One of the elders at the Church was talking to me about stuff and I was totally unable to cope with what he was saying. I stood up to leave and Malcolm came over and gave me a hug. The tears flowed yet again. Later on I sat down with Pete and admitted that I really wasn't right with God and that I needed to get it sorted. We spoke for some time and then Malcolm and Pete prayed for me. Eventually, after a week of being unable to pray, I came to God and prayed through the tears. Pete said that he felt he needed to tell me that in this brokenness not one piece was missing. I was reminded of my Ming vase that I had talked to Nic about a week earlier! The pool of tears on the table was mopped up. My heart touched and a sense that we had moved in the right direction.

So often as Christians we think that we should be able to manage alone, to just work through things with God. We actually need others. We are a people who need encouragement, hugs and sometimes people to come alongside and correct us. I know that I needed help to get right with God again. I couldn't do it on my own, and although admitting weakness, even sin, is hard and unnatural, for me it brought me out of a dark time. Yes, things were still hard and talking to God was still tentative, but we had turned a corner. For Malcolm this came days earlier than for me and he was able to make that progress on his own. However, I was too battered and broken which caused me to shut God out. I needed someone to come alongside to pray and help me weep before the Lord and confess my sin. I needed to confess my feelings and renew fellowship with Him.

The days and weeks after our miscarriage have been a real rollercoaster from grief to laughter, from despair to hope, from questioning God to accepting His plans. To start with the rollercoaster was extreme from one hour to the next. Seven weeks on and the rollercoaster is extreme from day to day or even week to week. The highs and the lows do not come so close together or quite so steeply.

Since we lost the baby we received tons of cards and flowers. Having been over three months pregnant the news had spread! The cards and flowers kept us going. We'd look at them and realize all the people who were praying for us and loved us! We've put them all in a folder to help us to remember, to thank God for that little life that one day we will meet.

It is strange really that through the years of infertility we envied those that miscarried because at least they knew they were able to conceive; but having been through this experience I can hardly believe that I ever felt that way. Since we lost our baby I have lost count of the number of people who have tried to 'comfort' us with the phrase 'at least you know you can conceive now.' This hasn't helped us at all even though as a couple we felt that way in the past when we looked at others. The realization that we may conceive again hardly comforts us in the fact that our first child has died.

Grief is a strange thing. When I lost my grandad I remembered happy times that would bring a smile to my face. I was so sad that he was no longer with us, but those happy memories really helped me. The strange thing about miscarriage is the happy memories are very limited because a large part of them are unseen. There is no set way to handle the loss of an unborn baby. A part of us is ripped away prematurely. I'm sure that no two people or no two couples handle it the same way.

For Malcolm and I it was more than losing a baby, it was losing the title of Mummy and Daddy, losing parenthood, even the right to be called a family. This was our first child. We do not know if we will have other children, especially in the light of our history. This simply has to be up to God. The heartache comes and goes. The rollercoaster rumbles on. Desperations can set in along with despair, but surely the key to managing all that this situation throws at us is to look at the one who 'lifts up those who are bowed down'. I read Psalm 145 yesterday and Psalm 146 today. I was struck by the repetition of this: in Psalm 145:14 it says, 'The LORD upholds all those who fall and lifts up all who are bowed down.' In Psalm 146:8 it says, 'the LORD gives sight to the blind, the LORD lifts up those who are bowed down, the LORD loves the righteous.'

It always intrigues me when something is repeated like this in Scripture – to me it shows that the Lord has a love for those who are broken and bowed down by life's circumstances. It encourages me that He does not simply want those that are doing well, those who are on fire for Him, those who are running well in the race of faith, but He wants those who are struggling, who cannot lift their heads, who are burdened, hurting and broken as well. What an awesome God we have! Whatever situation you are in as you read this, whether it is a high or a low in the rollercoaster, whether you are doing well or whether you are bowed down, the key is to look to the One who 'lifts up those who are bowed down'. He loves the broken-hearted. He loves those who don't fit into the mould that society has for them. He is the One who has compassion on the sinner. He cares for the weak and the suffering. He delights in us. Lift your gaze to Him. He surely is the answer.

This is a practical list of things that I wished we had been told about miscarriage. It is a list of things that I'm glad we were told, so I've decided to put them here – I hope they help! We are still learning, our miscarriage is still recent and we don't have all the answers. This is only what has happened in the early days after losing the baby.

I wish people had told us:

- *That each hour can be different, even each minute. I went from OK to devastated and back in short spaces of time.*

- *That the bleeding just goes on and on. On several occasions the clots were so massive that it felt*

171

that I was miscarrying all over again. To be honest the size of some of these scared me!

- *That my breasts would 'leak'. I had to phone a friend for breast pads because it was so bad.*

- *How empty I would feel.*

- *That it takes longer than you think to get over a miscarriage. Many people said to give it time but we had a certain expectation that it wouldn't take as long as it does!*

- *That people you hardly know will tell you their story of miscarriage, abortion or loss of a child.*

- *That you sometimes need to talk to someone from outside your marriage. That's OK. Both Malcolm and I have talked with others and also with others together. This isn't easy. I've never been good at being honest about how I feel, but I have learnt!*

What I'm glad people told us about miscarriage:

- *When I had questions about how long I would bleed for after the miscarriage several people at A&E told me different lengths of time.*

We heard about the miscarriage association so I phoned and asked them. They were so helpful. Some women bleed on and off for up to two weeks. The pain I got off and on was 'mini contractions' as I passed clots. Some days I would hardly bleed and others would be really heavy. This information from them was correct.

- *I am so glad I was told that it wasn't my fault and that it was the Lord who gave and it was the Lord that took away, therefore there was no need for me to feel a failure or ashamed.*

- *We were told to take our time. If you try to return to church, work, normality all at once it is overwhelming. Take mini-steps rather than giant leaps. I kept feeling it was all too much because I was trying to handle the next six months rather than the next six minutes.*

- *It was suggested that we give our baby a proper goodbye rather than just leaving it as it was. That night on Tower Bridge was so hard but in the days after we realized that it had brought an element of closure.*

- *Someone warned me that there would be people who wanted to know all the details and would ask blunt and personal questions. It still shocked me when it happened, but I'm glad I was warned!*

Miscarriage is a terrible thing to happen to anyone. I do not understand it and don't think that I ever will. But having said that, I know that I can trust God with all that has happened from the lowest moments to the highest. There is no one better to trust. He may take us along this road again or we may never become parents. I know that in whatever situation Malcolm and I find ourselves in – 'for this we have Jesus!'

13
Six Months After

So what about months after miscarriage? There have been times when I have been OK and there have also been times when I've struggled.

12th June

> ... I ache, I desperately long for Malcolm and I to be parents but it's just such a horrible thought at the same time. We would deal with the beginning of a pregnancy very differently now... after all that we've gone through since the beginning of the year. I feel confused, stressed and I'm hurting. My 'motherhood gene' throbs deep inside – longing to be in action. My brain aches with trying to sort out all my emotions along with longing to

be free from years of disappointment! My heart still weeps for my lost child. Everywhere I go I see women expecting and I have a regret deep inside that I'm no longer in that position. Expectation has turned to a brutal disappointment!

Can God heal these wounds that have been covered up, re-opened, enlarged, deepened so steadily over such a long period of time? I'm not sure whether I just need to come to terms with all that has happened. Whether I need to know healing for these wounds or whether somehow I just need to blot it all out and start afresh? How am I to handle this? I simply don't know.

I do know however what I don't want! I don't want to leave stuff un-dealt with. I've seen it in my life before and it's not pretty or helpful!

I was listening to 'Blessed Be Your Name' and 'This is the air I Breathe' as I vacuumed the Church today. I ended up in tears. I saw a picture of two sets of hands outstretched offering worship to God. In one pair of hands was a beautiful baby and in the other nothing! When I saw this I began to cry. But it was almost as though the Lord said that both offerings were good. The empty-handed offering that I bring is offered in pain but it's genuine from the heart. God just said, 'This is OK, I accept this offering!' Malcolm cried when I shared this with him!

15th June

*Why does this never get easier? This enormous
ache will never leave will it? Will I ever know
a freedom from infertility? It creeps around and
rears its ugly head when I am at my weakest.
Every time I seem to be getting there it looms
at the next turn. I want out of this situation so
much. Why can't God give me an 'easier lot in
life'? The tears don't flow so often, but the depth
of the ache is consuming again. I can't go down
the infertility treatment route again. It wouldn't
be fair on Malcolm or me. I love my dead baby.
The child I never saw and never knew. Every
time I see Jane's* child I will remember our baby.
It's so hard to take in. Why others and why not
us?*

*I have hit another point in my maze with
a dead end. All I want is a baby. Even today I
caught myself longing for a child rather than
God! I'm battling but I've really had enough of
this battle. The fight has gone on for too long.
Sometimes it has been too intense, too hard, and
I've felt that I will never survive it. I confess that
my emotions mean that I'm not thinking right,
but I can't ignore an ache that just won't go
away! I've had it! I've really had enough. Either
God has to answer my prayer or He has to give
me the grace and peace to go on. Either will do.*

---

* Name changed for obvious reasons

But I can't wait any longer. I'm not coping and it's eating away inside. I already feel pants about myself – useless, worthless etc…

I can't grasp what I should do. I don't understand where I go and I certainly can't go on like this! I'm sick of being OK, hitting a hurdle, sinking then God speaking and I start the whole thing again. I do need a permanent fix. I can't go on like this. I can't keep going to the same people with the same struggles, with a fresh lot of tears! The old 'Malcolm would be better off with someone else' has returned but I can't tell him because it would crush him! Permanent fix please Lord. I'm desperate for restoration, wholeness, completeness, healing, and peace. Just how can I get it?

16th June

We went to see Pete together after work. I've been struggling so much that Malcolm felt we should go! I didn't know what to say and was worried about going. Somehow we managed to talk stuff through. I need to be seeking God more than healing! The challenge is to talk to God about how I'm feeling! Malcolm and Pete prayed for me. It's a good job I was sitting down! I ended up not hearing them at all. It was just me and my Abba Father. He was just loving me, reassuring me that it's OK and calming my heart. It was good! I still ache – but it's not consuming. I still long but it's not my top desire! God has met me today!

3rd July

It's very late and I'm very tired. I should be asleep but my mind is racing! I really could do with someone to talk to but I can't wake up Malcolm – he is just so tired.

This week we had a mailing that had a car sign in it that said 'Mum-to-be on board' and 'Baby on board' on the other side. I coped OK and just dismissed it. But as the end of August gets nearer I realise that I'm not over losing our baby. Malcolm doesn't seem to want to talk about it and I am putting on a brave face – trying to be all I am supposed to be!

… Don't know what it is tonight but I can't stop thinking about our baby. I keep wondering about the 'what ifs', almost trying to imagine how I would feel now if I was seven and a half months pregnant. I know that I shouldn't think about it. I wish that somehow I could blot it out. Is it too much to ask to become a mum? Is it too much to ask to be normal? I'm aching and need to talk, but I can't. I need to cry with someone. I feel so alone right now. I don't want to be a pain or a bother to anyone, but I'm so desperate to share my ache!

I need to move on. I have to move on but how when my life is going to constantly be a 'what if' or an 'if only'? I can't see how I'm going to be able to move on when this is how my mind works! I guess guys and girls are very different.

Malcolm seems to have dealt with it and moved on. He's strong. Me? I'm a dreamer living in an unrealistic world of how I should be.

I know I'm tired. I know that Malcolm and I have been really busy lately. I know I'm weak and that we are under pressure from lots of different directions. This is simply a build up of all that and I must keep going. I cannot fail or let anyone down, but I can't help it. I just keep pressing on, keeping busy and then like tonight when I couldn't sleep I start to think and things fall apart. I wish I had the time to grieve, time for us, and time to be with my husband. The ache is too much tonight, I ache alone!

Our baby would have been due next month, yes NEXT month. Instead there is nothing … just us … doing all the stuff we are expected to be doing … this, that and the other. We're relied on for so much. I want to be me. I want to ache for my lost child but it feels like I'm not allowed to. It feels like I have to be super-human, but inside I'm broken and hurting. I'm so scared to let anyone see the inside. Scared to show people that I'm struggling all over again.

Why? Why me?

I don't want to be patched up anymore. I just want to be a mum – please!

Malcolm woke after I wrote this and we wept together, prayed together and returned to bed together. We lay there and talked together and ached together. The next day we both felt so raw. Months had passed since the miscarriage and yet we still grieved for one we never saw and one we never knew, but for one that we love totally.

Several people who had experienced miscarriage suggested that we named our baby, at the time I dismissed it – we were content to stick with the nickname 'Peanut.' However months after we lost the baby, even after the due date I really began to struggle that our baby was not classed as a person, our baby didn't have a proper name. It was about a month after the due date that I wrote Malcolm a long letter, I was really struggling and hadn't really been able to talk to him – in this letter I asked him if we could name the baby – our lives had a real hole in them. We no longer had lost something (the pregnancy) we really felt that we had lost someone, our baby. There was a physical gap in our lives now – someone that should have been there wasn't. It was over a fortnight later that we named our baby standing on Brighton Beach during a weekend away. My diary for that day shows how key that step was for us:-

Saturday 17th September

*We've talked much today over stuff on and off.
We walked down to the beach this evening – it was
dark except for the street and pier lights. We stood
together at the edge of the sea with the waves
lapping and chatted. We talked about whether our
baby's character would have been decided already.
And then we did it – we confirmed together the
name of our baby – Abigail Ruth-Anne – the
girl's name that we chose back in 1997. We
prayed together committing Abigail Cameron
to the Lord, committing our future to the Lord
and also ourselves to Him afresh. We did business
with God on the beach this evening. It has really
helped me to hear Malcolm call our baby Abigail
– I can't describe it really – there is a kind of
finality – not a bad one, a good one alongside is a
peace that we have made our decision. Our baby
will not be known as 'Peanut' but as Abigail
– peanut was merely a nickname – Abigail Ruth-
Anne is her name. This weekend away has been
vital. I also prayed on the beach that God would
help us through the grief and give me courage to
face the stuff that simply feels unfaceable at the
moment.*

People say that pregnancy and childbirth alter
your life dramatically. Everything changes. For
us we discovered that a pregnancy followed by

miscarriage does exactly the same. Miscarriage is not like the flu. With the flu you recover from the physical effects and months later forget that you were ever under the weather. As I write this it is five months after I miscarried and I cannot believe how raw the ache still is. I admit that there have been highs and lows over these last months, but as the due date looms – things are very hard. Seven months ago we were thrilled about this date and now we dread it.

Our lives have been dramatically changed by what happened at the beginning of this year. Everything changed and has changed again. What do I mean? Well our plans changed drastically. We'd thought through maternity leave, our summer, Malcolm's holiday and paternity leave. The excitement over what was going to happen changed drastically from having to make plans to plans that were no longer required. Our excitement was lost and normal was so unwanted!

As the due date draws closer I have found it harder to talk to people. I've felt that no one understands. I have had this expectation that I should be further along, coping better, stronger and not needing to cry, and yet there has come a point where we have had to talk and cry and be honest – even though it's hard. I've been back to that same place of brokenness time and time again over the past months, sometimes alone, sometimes with Malcolm, sometimes with trusted friends or family. The loss of our child is acute, the 'what ifs' have been rampant, the reminders painful. Even last week we had to go to the loft for something and I caught sight of a couple of boxes packed up. The tears were there instantly. The depth of heartache is hard to put into words. But there have been blessings too. Last week a work colleague gently and lovingly said that they knew the time was drawing near and assured me that they were there for me. Our pastor has again said that it's OK to cry and to hurt, even though I get so frustrated with myself. I guess over the last few weeks and even for the next few weeks that word assurance is key. There is the total assurance that God knows, that He cares and that my standing in Him has not changed because my motherhood role has!

It is still not easy. We still struggle. We still cry. We sometimes still feel angry. We still hurt. We still battle. We still ache and we still cry again. But in all those 'stills' we also still know that our God reigns, that He is still sovereign, that He can still be trusted, that He is still in control, that He still loves us, that He still promises good things for those He loves and that when we are broken He still knows.

It's easy to say this as I sit at my computer on a warm summer's evening, but even yesterday it would have been a battle to speak such truth because grief consumed and the enemy pressed in hard. Yes, today I still ache, I still wish that things were different; but the realization comes afresh that it's one step at a time, even when there are knock-backs and tough days, that there is One who we can look to for help, who lifts us up and cares in the bleakest of days. We need to stand firm on the truth of who we are in Christ and all that He has achieved for us with a reality that isn't simply positive thinking but reaches our hearts and fixes our gaze afresh upon our totally awesome God.

14
NICK'S PRAYER AFTER THE MISCARRIAGE

Firstly, let me share with you the background to this prayer and why Malcolm and I felt it so important to put it in this book. It was only the third night after the miscarriage. On nights one and two I had woken just before 3am and not been able to return to sleep. This night I was exhausted physically, spiritually and emotionally. I was tossing and turning trying to sleep and realized that Malcolm was being disturbed yet again. I knew that he needed to sleep so I got up! I sat on the rocking chair in our dining room with paper and pen. I had tried to pray but couldn't voice the words. Tears rolled down my cheeks and I decided to write my prayer down. This is simply what I wrote. At one point I was so overcome, my crying woke Malcolm who came down, gave me a hug and some toast, and then returned to bed! It was at this break that my gaze was lifted and in the anguish the glimmer of hope came. The prayer changed at this point, as you will see. When I had finished writing it for the first time in days I was able to return to bed with peace in my heart and head. I went straight back to sleep. My focus was not on the hopelessness but on a God who brought peace and who was still worthy despite what had happened. We thought we should share this very personal prayer with you because God used it not only on that night but also in the days after the miscarriage – we pray that it helps you too.

Prayer written on 29/2/04 at 3.30 am (72 hours after the miscarriage):

Dear Lord, my heart is broken, my baby is gone, my hopes are dashed, dreams smashed into tiny pieces. I can hardly speak for the lump in my throat. Each tear hurts like a stabbing wound. I simply don't understand so I come confused, weary and broken to the core. There is disappointment yet again. Emptiness consumes me; loneliness overwhelms even when there are people around. Darkness abounds. In the midst of the pain I cry out to you. There seems no response but I think my grief covers my ears allowing nothing to be heard – the hollow sound of agony!

The words 'Mummy' and 'Daddy' that Malcolm and I have called one another now and again no longer relevant – no longer apply. The bump that I had lovingly stroked each night, caressing through my own flesh the tiny life inside, now no longer seems beautiful – an empty expanse, a void. The precious gift that I already loved with all my heart; that I treasured is snatched to the grave. Our child – never seen, never touched, never heard, never named but so loved – the un-believableness of it shakes me to the core of my being. I feel like I have withered and died. The frost is simply too harsh for this fragile one. I long for the summer sunshine – for warmth again.

Yet in the anguish there is a glimmer of hope, in the despair a comfort. You, O Lord – you never change. Your love does not alter. You are still good. Some would say that is a bizarre thing to say at a time like this – but it's true. You are unchanging therefore you are always good. Simply because I have experienced the horrors of the night does not change your characteristics. You are still faithful and true. You are still a God of love and all comfort and you are unchanging in your worthiness. You O Lord are so worthy, worthy of adoration, worthy of worship, worthy of praise. Let my shouts not be of accusation, anger or terror.

Let my shouts be of delight again in my loving Saviour; my Father God; the one who takes the hand of my child and smiles over them; the one who knows my heart's desires; the one who knows my longings, the one who sees each tear and knows my every thought. In my heartache let me not take my eyes off of you or your beauty, your delight in me.

Let my heart not be consumed by emptiness but renewed passion, a fresh delight in you. Come Lord. Fill this fragile, broken vessel. Touch the core of my being. Let me feel your healing touch. I choose to praise you. I choose to seek your face. I choose not to look at the hopelessness of my current situation and wallow in self-pity. I choose to look up. I choose to praise your worthy name. Yes, there is pain in the offering that I bring. Yes, I still weep and struggle. Yes, I still long to hold our child.

I anticipate the day where I will gaze upon the face of my own son or daughter to touch their fingers and caress their toes but this is not the only thing that I desire, that I crave. I long too for the touch of your Spirit, the healing grace that only flows from you. I long for the unmistakable touch of your Spirit, flowing over me again, refreshing, revitalizing and capturing my heart again. Yes the tears still flow and the ache still throbs but I WILL still praise you for your worthiness has not changed.

15
THE MEDICINE OF PRAISE AND PRAYER

The first thing to say as I begin this chapter is that I have no idea how people cope with infertility and miscarriage without knowing the Lord. Again and again over the years this has 'blown my mind'. I just can't get my head round how people live through such times without knowing Him. I know that for us the initial years were really desperate. I know that there have been times when we have lost all hope of ever having children. I have in the past asked people to stand with me in prayer for a restoration of hope! There have been times, and this may, or may not, shock you, where I have felt that I can't go on. Yes, I have felt suicidal. On some occasions this was obvious to Malcolm. At other times it wasn't. But in the darkest of hours, the most hopeless of times and in the intensity of brokenness there has been Someone that I have clung to. The LORD has been my refuge and my strength, my ever-present help in trouble. Yes, it's from Psalm 46:1! And it doesn't just stop there. The whole Psalm is great! Verse 2 goes on to say, 'Therefore we will not fear, though the earth give way and the mountains fall into the heart of the sea'.

In my Bible seven little words are scrawled in the margin. These words have made a difference so many times: 'Though everything solid may collapse God doesn't.' This really has been my testimony in the lowest of times, just when everything seems to be collapsing around me, my hope gone and despair is all I see. I remember these seven words and cry out to my ever-present help!

I know that God has seen me through. I know that there have been times that I have cried out to Him, 'Where are you?' It's then that I've picked up my Bible and read something that has spoken to me right where I'm at. At other times the phone has rung, an e-mail has arrived or a text message has been received – and God has blessed them. God has used friends and family at opportune moments to assure me that He is there and that He does care.

The Medicine of Praise

But this chapter title talks about medicine. What medicine? Well firstly we have medicine of praise. I am so glad that in this day and age God has inspired men and women all over the world to write songs that have helped me so much! In some ways I would love to write them out in full for you to read afresh the words and let them flow over your pain as they have for me. These are songs like: *For this I have Jesus*; *What a Faithful God have I*; *I've had Questions*.

Just read these awesome words from *Before the throne of God above* by C. L. S. Bancroft:

When Satan tempts me to despair
And tells me of the guilt within
Upward I look and see Him there
Who made an end to all my sin.

The hymn *To be In Your Presence* has a line that says: 'Where your love surrounds me and makes me complete.'

I love the song *Blessed Be Your Name*, as the chorus meant more to us after the miscarriage. It was Job 1: 21b in song for us: 'You give and take away, my heart will choose to say Lord blessed be your name.'

The list of songs is in fact endless, there are so many, these are just a handful that spring to mind!

I have never been able to sing 'For this I have Jesus' without crying. The words of the verses are the echo of my heart:

For the joys and for the sorrows,
The best and worst of times,
For this moment, for tomorrow,
For all that lies behind;
Fears that crowd around me,
For the failure of my plans,
For the dreams of all I hope to be,
The truth of what I am:

For this I have Jesus,
For this I have Jesus,
For this I have Jesus,
I have Jesus.

For the tears that flow in secret,
In the broken times,
For the moments of elation,
Or the troubled time;
For all the disappointments,
Or the sting of old regrets,
All my prayers and longings
That seem unanswered yet:

For the weakness of my body,
The burdens of each day,
For the nights of doubt and worry,
When sleep has fled away;
Needing reassurance,
And the will to start again,
A steely-eyed endurance,
The strength to fight and win:

By Graham Kendrick

Yes, the whole song is my experience but the chorus reminds me that it is for these times that I have Jesus, it points me back to Him – my Jesus whom I have for the best and the worst of times. Yes, these songs and many others have spoken to me in a situation that can consume and overwhelm if you take your eyes off God.

Worship CDs are a lifeline when you are trying to call out to God and you don't seem to be getting anywhere. OK, so Malcolm and I love music. The sound of silence is not often heard in our house! However, there have been times, for example after the miscarriage where in the middle of the night I just played the song 'I've Had Questions' very quietly on repeat for ages. It doesn't always need to be loud! This song has ministered to my heart time and time again so much so that I just need to put it here for you to read:

I've had questions, without answers.
I've known sorrow. I have known pain
But there's one thing that I'll cling to:
You are faithful. Jesus you are true.

When hope is lost, I'll call you Saviour.
When pain surrounds, I'll call you healer.
When silence falls, you'll be the song
Within my heart.

In the lone hour of my sorrow,
Through the darkest night of my soul,
You surround me and sustain me,
My defender, forever more.

I will praise you. I will praise you.
When the tears fall, still I will sing to you.
I will praise you, Jesus praise you,
Through the suffering still I will sing.

By Tim Hughes

I sat that night listening to this song repeatedly. I listened. I wept and in my anguish my broken spirit echoed these words. My offering of praise that night was in brokenness and through tears.

There have been other times when we have been going through very difficult times and Malcolm has come down the stairs and caught me dancing before the Lord (not a pretty sight), but a testimony that I've gone from perplexed to praise, from despair to delight!

Praise and worship are of vital importance in our walk with the Lord. I am not referring to just saying words or singing songs. Praise is when you really enter in. It is an awesome experience. Nothing around seems to matter and you stand there 'warts and all', just you and the One that you adore. So often we see worship as a mere sing song, a nice vocal time, with catchy tunes and foot-tapping melodies. We see the outward bits as worship and simply go through the motions sometimes with our minds caught up on what someone else is wearing, their new haircut or on our next meal! We need to engage not only our bodies and voices, but also our minds, our spirits our innermost thoughts. How can we ever worship God fully if we aren't even thinking about Him? Praise and worship does not have to be sung either. We can whisper, talk or shout praise. To be a real worshipper is not just about singing or whatever, it is actually a way of life!

I learnt early on that praise was going to be key in living through infertility and it was a close friend who pointed out Psalm 119:164. It was during a time where my focus was very blurred and I was kind of pointing in the wrong direction. But this verse refers to praising God seven times a day. My friend suggested that I should wear seven bangles and that the noise of them would remind me to praise God. During the day I would move these bangles from one wrist to the other as a reminder to praise. There were some tough days in those first years of infertility that you would catch me wearing seven bangles (and sometimes a few more)!

There have been countless times when I have been struggling in the depths, unable to pull myself out, and I've put on a CD, been in a prayer meeting or at a service. Then as I have heard what is sung, prayed or said it is almost as if there is an elevator in the depths. I climb on board and hit the 'up' button as I've sung truth and heard of my Lord, and the elevator has risen. The doors on the elevator open as I recognize the truth about my God. I declare it aloud and I find myself delighting in God, at a new height. The depths seem small and insignificant in light of the awesome One that I am praising. This is not about the power of positive thinking. This is about the power of praise thinking. It's about not looking at the disappointments, but looking at the awesome

God. We see loads of times in Scripture where people have been in really tough situations and they have started to look to God and ended up praising! Just read the Psalms or Lamentations chapter 3 if you don't believe me!

One of the biggest temptations I have experienced is the temptation to think that I've been 'left on the shelf' or just plain forgotten. This is an ongoing toughie, even now as I write this I battle with it! But this is a hard challenge we face. How do we counteract such negative thoughts? It is simple, but hard to do when you are hurting. We need to fill our minds with truth! For example, when you are feeling, 'God's forgotten me', think on this: Could the one who created you, who knew you in your mother's womb, who sent His only Son to die for you, who chose you, who knows every single hair of your head, who knows everything about you, who loves you unconditionally, who accepts you as you are, who has prepared a place for you in heaven – could this One who has done all this for you just forget about you? Never!

I have repeatedly put myself down. I've told myself that I'm a useless, worthless failure. OK, imagine if I said that to myself every day – how would I feel? You've guessed it – I would feel that I'm a useless, worthless failure. OK, imagine that if every day I declared how good God is, that He is a God who is faithful, reliable, loving and true – how would I feel? Well, my focus wouldn't be on me or my situation so much would it? It would be on God!

The Medicine of Prayer

Now let's get onto the medicine of prayer. I am so glad that we are able to talk to God directly. I am so glad that we do not have to go through other people to talk to Him and tell Him how we are feeling. It has taken me a long time to learn to be honest with God. Barmy isn't it? He already knows our every thought, our every situation, our every feeling, but we still struggle to tell Him these things! I am so pleased that I have my Lord. My God is always there. He does not slumber or sleep. Yes, there have been times when I have been unable to talk to Him, completely unable to speak. There have been times where the darkness has closed in so much that I haven't been able to see past it. Talking to God is not easy when you are going through rough times, but if we persevere and are not put off we will come to a place where it is easier to talk to Him.

Others have been used to spiritually take me by the hand and lead me to a place where I have been able to talk to the Lord. Sometimes it has taken a bit of a loving kick in the right direction from Malcolm to get me to pray. At other times someone completely different has challenged me. Sometimes it has been my daily times with the Lord that have moved me on. I confess when it comes to praying I'm not very good at doing it alone. I'm rubbish at it in fact! I have a brain that will pray and concoct a 'to-do list' at the same time – arrgghh! I admit that the best time for me to pray alone is when Malcolm is out and I can pray about anything I want out loud. If I pray alone I have to speak it out, otherwise the list of jobs takes over and I just don't get anywhere!

Prayer is a lifeline for hurting people – I know it, I've seen it, I've experienced it – prayer is key. I praise God that we had people around us who never said, 'We've prayed about this before, this ground is covered – sort yourself out!'

In the past it took months to pluck up enough courage to ask someone to pray for me, but God has now given me a boldness that I didn't have before. I can go up to someone and just ask for prayer now. I always thought that asking someone to pray or going forward for prayer in response to a message was a failure, showing weakness. I thought it showed that my faith was not strong or mature. There have been times when I have been to the same person and asked them to pray about the same thing! Several times in fact! I always end up apologizing that I haven't done better and that I'm back in that same place again. Some very good friends have had astonishing patience in praying for me and with me in the broken times! I praise God that He created us to be part of a family, the Body of Christ!

Then there are those times when we ask God but struggle to believe that the answer will come! For seven and a half years we prayed for a baby and then we discovered that I was pregnant. We were quite shocked! I love Psalm 5:3 which says, 'In the morning, O LORD, you hear my voice; in the morning I lay my requests before you and wait in expectation.' We have an awesome God, we should be expectant of the awesome things that He will do! I'm not saying that we should pray and then simply sit back and expect to get pregnant just like that because we have asked. But if we are praying for things in line with God's will then we should expect great things in His timing!

My husband astounds me with his faith when he prays, but especially when he prays for the children and young people that we work with in our church. He'll pray something that I agree with and I think, 'Oh that would be awesome if it happened.' But the difference is I think 'if' – Malcolm prays and thinks 'when'! Sometimes we need an injection of faith in our prayer life!

To conclude this book I want to take you to Isaiah 61. I love this entire chapter for many reasons, one being that an old school principal referred many times to the 'Oaks of Righteousness'. However, this chapter is primarily about our God who has a love and concern for the broken-hearted and about how we should delight in Him.

There are two particular phrases in this chapter that I really love. The first is in verse 7 where it says that 'Instead of their shame my people will receive a double portion'. This reminds me of the story of Hannah who had shame because of her infertility and yet her husband, Elkanah, loved her so much that he gave her a double portion (1 Sam. 1:5). Often I feel that shame because of infertility, but I know that the Lord loves me and so I anticipate the double portion (whatever that means)! The other phrase is in verse 3 'a garment of praise instead of a spirit of despair'. This is my heart's cry as I have often had a spirit of despair. Although sometimes it comes and goes, I long for my life to be clothed in a garment of praise!

There does not seem to be an adequate way to end this book. Mine is a story that is not complete. I have no happy ending in relation to us having children. I'm not sure what the future holds on that score. I do not understand God's ways and why certain things happen to certain people. However, I do know that my heart's cry to God, even after all that we have been through, is simply two words, 'Whatever Lord.' I know there will be tough days ahead. The rollercoaster will have exhilarating highs and stomach-churning lows, but whatever happens, 'I know whom I adore. I believe in him and He will not let me down.'

Dear friend, hold fast on the rollercoaster you are on. Keep going. Press onwards and upwards. Revel afresh in knowing Jesus and be astounded afresh with His love.

May the God of hope fill you with all joy and peace as you trust in him, so that you may overflow with hope by the power of the Holy Spirit (Rom. 15:13).

16
LETTER FROM NICK

Dear Friend,

In the midst of the ache that you are
feeling right now I pray that you will see
the Creator's hand upon your life, His
arms around you and His comforting
touch. I know that at the moment the
entire world seems to revolve around
having a baby. I know that the feeling
is crushing and life seems unbearable.
When the ache is intense and the tears
flow, it seems that laughter will never
return and brokenness consumes, but
in that ache there is a loving God who

cares. There is One who will consume with a new passion. There is One who knows every tear shed, every thought, every heart's desire and every cry that you utter.

He longs to meet you right where you are. He longs to meet you whether you are in joy or whether you are in despair. He craves to be with you. He longs to be with you. He loves the times that you spend together. Call on His name. Praise this awesome God. Be in His presence and be surprised once again with all that He has done for you. Our God is not a distant God. He is near at hand. His fountain of grace and healing oil are always there for you. When you are desperate, aching and you just want to collapse, then fall at the feet of the supreme Lover, come to your healer God and let Him minister afresh His love and grace into your life. When it never seems that healing will come, stand firm with a determination that is not fired by desires or stubbornness but that is fired from a confidence in the Almighty God and His Holy Spirit dwelling within you.

Whether this road is long or short,

whether there is an answer, a wait or a question mark, look to Him. Let your delight be in Him. Love His Word. Gaze upon His beauty. Be amazed at His wonders and enjoy knowing Him as well as being known by Him.

Dear friend, 'When hope is lost call Him Saviour. When pain surrounds call Him Healer.'

In Jesus,

Nick

If you would like to contact Malcolm or Nick please use the address below:

Malcolm & Nick Cameron
c/o Lansdowne Evangelical Church
Lansdowne Hill
West Norwood
London
SE27 0AR

Website: www.hopewhenithurts.co.uk
E-mail: info@hopewhenithurts.co.uk